Jane L. Thompson

STUDYING SOCIETY

Hutchinson of London

Hutchinson & Co. (Publishers) Ltd
3 Fitzroy Square, London W1P 6JD

London Melbourne Sydney Auckland
Wellington Johannesburg and agencies
throughout the world

First published 1978
Reprinted 1978

Set in IBM Pyramid

Printed in Great Britain by The Anchor Press Ltd
and bound by Wm Brendon & Son Ltd
both of Tiptree, Essex

ISBN 0 09 129241 7

CONTENTS

ACKNOWLEDGEMENTS

The author and publisher are grateful to the following for their permission to reproduce textual material:

Social Trends published by HMSO: pp. 19-26, 52, 92-94; *Daily Express:* pp. 27 (13 May '75), 70; NSPCC: pp. 36, 114, 115; Routledge & Kegan Paul Ltd: pp. 42, 59, 82; *Statistics of Education* published by HMSO: 53; Peter Davies Ltd: p. 53; Labour Party: p. 53; *Where* published by ACE: p. 56; *Jackie:* p. 65; Macmillan Education Ltd: p. 65; Ward Lock Educational Co. Ltd: p. 67; Fontana: p. 67; Mainman Ltd/Chrysalis Music/Bowie: p. 68; Cambridge University Press: p. 68; Calder & Boyars Ltd: p. 68; Paladin: pp. 69-70; *Daily Telegraph:* p. 70; *Daily Mirror:* pp. 70, 96 (14 Jan '75); *The Sun* (13 May '75): p. 74; *New Society* (17 Feb '72): p. 89; Hart-Davis Educational Ltd: p. 97; SCM Press Ltd: p. 98; *The Guardian* (5 Dec '75); pp. 99-100; *Woman:* p. 101; Open University: pp. 60, 107; Blond & Briggs Ltd: p. 119; George Allen & Unwin Ltd: p. 130; Faber & Faber Ltd: p. 143; Times Newspapers Ltd: pp. 143, 144; © *New Left Review* 1967, 1968, by permission of Penguin Books Ltd: pp. 145-6; *Observer:* p. 147; *Sunday Express* (13 July '75): p. 151; I.B.A.: p. 153.

We are also grateful to the following for their permission to reproduce illustrations:

The Mansell Collection: p. 23; Keystone Press: pp. 23, 30, 31, 54, 58, 70, 116, 142; Barnaby's Picture Library: pp. 28, 43, 69, 77, 89, 105, 110, 118, 122, 123, 149, 155; Anchor Housing Association: p. 29; Oxfam Youth Department: p. 28; Camera Press: 29, 58, 71, 102, 103, 113, 123, 141; Popperfoto: pp. 30, 70, 156; Gravesend & Dartford Reporter: p. 37; G.A. Clark: p. 38; Jane Thompson: pp. 42, 80, 81, 104, 125; Janine Wiedel: p. 42; Times Newspapers Ltd: p. 43; Greater London Council: pp. 46, 104, 125; Socialist Woman : p. 53; London Express News & Feature Services: p. 67; Robert Ellis: p. 66; Health Education Council: p. 79; Nick Hedges: pp. 80, 81, 95, 112, 124; Family Planning Association: p. 82; Anglo-Chinese Educational Institute: pp. 98, 99; George Wimpey & Co. Ltd: p. 104; T.H. Williams: p. 105; Shelter: p. 112; Roger Mayne: pp. 113, 127, 136; Aerofilms: p. 122; Radio Times Hulton Picture Library: pp. 123, 127; Wates Ltd: p. 125; Noel Coombes: p. 126; Laurence Sparham (IFL): p. 140; Metropolitan Police: p. 140; Stan Newens: p. 145; Chris Davies (Report): p. 147; B.B.C. Photos: 157; Henry Grant: pp. 30, 47, 48, 50, 57, 78, 80, 81, 113, 126, 156; *Evening Standard:* pp 156, 157.
Cartoons drawn by Martin Williams.

Every effort has been made to reach copyright holders, but the publisher would be grateful to hear from any source whose copyright they may unwittingly have infringed.
The author would like to thank Mike Shellens for his help with Chapter 2, and Pat Wilson for typing the original manuscript.

TEACHERS' FOREWORD

Studying Society deliberately sets out to interest and involve pupils taking Social Studies and Humanities course for CSE.

The emphasis is on pupil activity and through a variety of approaches helps to develop the skills of information gathering, interpretation, imagination, illustration and discussion, in an enjoyable and lively way.

Each chapter introduces a separate theme, such as childhood or community concerns, and is made up of a series of related topics. In each case a photograph, newspaper cutting, chart or case-study provides the stimulus. Then carefully structured questions and suggestions help the pupils to develop and investigate the topics in greater depth.

Each chapter ends with a Top Ten page to check terms and information used earlier in the text, Discussion Starters, Project Starters and Social Action Starters. These are deliberately geared to the specific requirements of CSE examinations and provide a range of follow-up work which pupils can pursue individually or collectively.

Studying Society is meant to be a working book, pupil-centred and activity-based. But it also includes a wealth of information from a wide variety of sources. Although the teacher's main concern will be to guide pupils to appropriate resources and through relevant information (and the list of addresses on p. 160 may be useful here), the teacher will undoubtedly need to direct some pupils towards certain topics rather than others and to exercise a good deal of control over the depth and quality of their pupils' work.

There are many text-books which present pre-digested information for pupils to regurgitate, but *Studying Society* aims to be different. It is a unique attempt to combine enjoyable and stimulating learning activities with the serious demands of external and Mode III examinations. If it succeeds it should help teachers to convince their pupils that learning can be both informative and exciting.

Jane L Thompson

1 STUDYING SOCIETY

Take a good look at yourself!

What makes you tick? What kind of person are you — friendly? bad-tempered? super-intelligent? light-hearted? cheeky? ambitious? modest? What do you like doing? How do you spend your spare time? Do you get on well at school or college? What are you going to do when you leave? What will you be like in ten years' time? Thirty years' time?

What do you think about these people? What do you know about them? Are they like you, or different? What makes you and them the kinds of people you are?

The way to find out the answers to questions like these is by studying SOCIETY and by looking very closely at some of the things which happen in society. Most of them have an important effect on the kinds of people we are.

7

GROUPS AND ROLES

Animals live in herds, birds live in flocks, and people live in GROUPS. From the second we are born, and throughout our lives, we are claimed by a number of different groups — our family and relatives, school friends and work-mates, members of the same club or team, our trade union or our neighbours. All of them help to look after us, bring us up, influence us or control us at different times in our life.

Like the rest of us, young Fred belongs to quite a few different groups. If you were to ask him, 'What kind of person are you?' a variety of different pictures of himself might flash through his mind.

Family group	Football team	Church choir	Youth club	School class	Supermarket

Son	Footballer	Choirboy	Youth club member	Pupil	Saturday-boy

In each of these groups he plays a slightly different part. A bit like an actor — except that each part goes much deeper than a performance in a play. Taken together, they make him the complete person he is. We use an 'acting' term to describe these different parts. We call them ROLES.

YOUR OWN EXPERIENCE

1 Make a list of the different groups to which you belong.
2 Make a list of the different groups to which your mother or father belongs.
3 Which groups do you both belong to, and which of these are different?
4 In the family group you play the role of son or daughter and perhaps brother or sister. As a son or daughter you may have to do as your parents say, maybe help with certain household chores, possibly keep an eye on younger brothers or sisters.
   a) Describe what you do to play your role in the family.
   b) Explain how your mother's or father's role in the family differs from yours.
   c) Describe the role you play in each of the other groups to which you belong.

People in different groups expect different things of him. That's all right so long as he keeps the roles separate. But sometimes he finds himself being asked to play two different roles at the same time. Should he do his Saturday job of stocking shelves in the supermarket or go off to play in an important football match for the school? Should he be 'the baby of the family' to please his mother, or a 'trendy young man' to please his friends?

This kind of conflict situation, that we all get into from time to time, is called ROLE CONFLICT. Imagine a teacher with her own son in the class; or a policeman who finds his daughter taking drugs; or a doctor banned for drunken driving; or a woman torn between her family and her career. All of these involve two or more of a person's roles conflicting with each other.

1 Describe any role conflicts you have experienced in playing your different roles of son or daughter, pupil and teenager.
2 Explain the role conflict for the teacher, the policeman, the doctor and the woman in the examples above.

As you work through this book you will learn quite a lot about the different roles played by people in society at different times in their lives, and about how these roles are affected by the different groups they belong to in society. You will learn that each person is an individual, and different from everyone else, but that some people, who are members of the same SEX or RACE or SOCIAL CLASS, have important things in common.

You'll see that some of the things we tend to 'take for granted' and think of as 'natural' — like the different roles played by men and women in society — are in fact 'man-made'. People don't have different ATTITUDES and behave in different ways because of 'human nature' — or at least, not very much. Their attitudes and BEHAVIOUR depend much more on the kind of society they are brought up in.

In this book you will be studying how society influences their behaviour. The proper word for this kind of study is SOCIOLOGY, and for the people who study it, SOCIOLOGISTS.

WHY STUDY SOCIETY?

Sociologists are interested to find out how and why people behave as they do, because it helps them to understand people better. This means asking questions, doing INVESTIGATIONS and trying to find reasons for people's actions. This may seem nosey to you. Sociologists are often accused of prying into things that don't concern them. But many of the things that happen in society aren't good. The behaviour of some people makes life difficult for others. And only by finding out the facts can we hope to make society a better place for everyone.

A TOUCH OF CLASS

'No longer true,' you might say. 'We don't look up to some people and look down on others just because of their social class. All people are equal in Britain. One person is just as good as the next.'

Of course you're right. These PREJUDICED ideas about social class are out of date. It's much more difficult to tell people's social class just by looking at them these days and most people don't believe that one class is better than another any more. But differences do exist. Most of us believe ourselves to be either working class or middle class and when we use these terms about others we have a fairly clear picture in our minds of what we mean by them.

Look carefully at this list of characteristics:

1 Which of them do you think are most typical of upper class people today?
2 Which are most typical of middle class people today?
3 Which are most typical of working class people today?
4 Which could be equally true of any class?

Attends the Church of England regularly
Reads *The Times*
Keep pigeons in the back garden
Plays polo
Drives a Mini
Owns a semi-detached house in the suburbs
Wears hand-tailored clothes
Reads the *Daily Mirror*
Has been educated at university
Drives a Rolls-Royce
Drinks a pint of mild
Takes holidays in the south of France
Lives in rented accommodation
Plays Bingo
Sends children to public school
Takes holidays in Blackpool
Enjoys classical music
Owns two or more houses
Watches rugby union
Drinks scotch on the rocks

When you've finished your lists discuss them together with your teacher.

1 Which characteristics did you all agree were typical of upper class, middle class and working class people?
2 Which characteristics did you disagree about most?
3 Suggest reasons why there should be so much agreement over some characteristics and so much disagreement over others.

When sociologists are deciding people's social class they usually go by the kind of job they do and the amount of money they have. But sociologists also take into account people's education, the kind of house in which they live, what interests and hobbies they have, how they spend their leisure time and what attitudes they have to life. This information is used to put people into one of seven categories and sociologists say that people in the same category tend to have the same kind of jobs, amount of money, education, interests, attitudes and way of life in common.

These are the seven categories:

UPPER CLASS   Aristocracy and large property owners

UPPER MIDDLE CLASS Professional occupations e.g. lawyers and architects

MIDDLE CLASS Managerial and technical jobs e.g. shop managers and computer operators.

LOWER MIDDLE CLASS Non-manual, white-collar and clerical jobs e.g. office workers and supervisors.

UPPER WORKING CLASS   Skilled manual jobs e.g. electricians and vehicle mechanics.

WORKING CLASS Semi-skilled manual jobs e.g. machine operators and trawler-men

LOWER WORKING CLASS Unskilled manual jobs e.g. road sweepers and canteen assistants

There are obviously exceptions to the rule, and as you go through life you'll probably meet lots of people who don't seem to fit the category sociologists would put them in. But in general the categories are fairly accurate and they provide a useful way of identifying different groups of people in society who have important things in common. We'll look at some of these in more detail later in the book.

USING THIS BOOK

As you work through the book, you'll see that every chapter has Project Starters, Discussion Starters and a Top Ten. Look out for Social Action Starters, too. You'll soon get the hang of them, but here are a few things to keep in mind.

This symbol represents the *TOP TEN* and comes near to the end of each chapter. There are ten questions, each one needing a one-word answer, or a sentence at the most.

In most cases you should know the answers from the work you've already done. So this is a way of testing your memory.

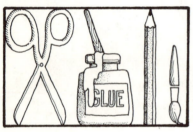

This symbol marks the *DISCUSSION STARTERS* page. This is an opportunity for you to talk about what you've learned or to give your opinion on some important issue. You might even have to make a speech to the rest of the class.

Discussion Starters are useful because it's important that you learn to speak up for yourself. It's good practice for the future, for interviews, for putting your point of view in an argument and for dealing with various officials.

This symbol means *PROJECT STARTERS*. At the end of each chapter you'll find a number of pictures and suggestions about projects you might like to do. This is an opportunity for you to choose something which interests you and to follow it up in as lively and interesting a way as you can. The Project Starters will give you an idea. How you follow it up depends on you. But here are three things to remember:

1 Projects can be written but they don't have to be. Photographs, drawings, films, slides, tape-recordings, plays, models, graphs and charts are just some of the different approaches you can use. A good project would probably include two or three of these approaches.
2 Make full use of what you've learned about, using the library, asking questions, writing letters, doing surveys, interviews and questionnaires.
3 Don't copy passages out of books. In most cases your own drawings and photographs are better than pictures cut out of magazines.

This symbol means *SOCIAL ACTION STARTERS*. It's a good idea to put your studies to some practical use whenever you can. Social Action Starters give you the opportunity to do this. They're suggestions of ways in which you can take some action in the neighbourhood, during school time or after school, to help local residents.

It might be possible for your teacher to arrange other Social Action activities besides those mentioned in the book, for example, working in a children's play-group or designing and making special aids for handicapped people. You'll probably have a few ideas yourself.

Always keep a diary to record what you do.

FINDING OUT FOR YOURSELF

As you use this book you'll find that it doesn't *tell* you very much. But it helps you to find things out for yourself, if you know the right approach. Start with information supplied in this book then start thinking of sources further afield. In most cases you'll be given something to start you off. It might be an EXTRACT, a NEWSPAPER CUTTING, a PHOTOGRAPH, a CARTOON or some STATISTICS.

Important words or special terms used by sociologists in this book are introduced in capital letters. Make sure you understand them. Always check the GLOSSARY (p. 158) if you don't.

Each time you come across an EXTRACT (see p. 67)

1 read it carefully.
2 make sure you understand all the difficult words.
3 ask about anything you don't understand.

Each time you read a NEWSPAPER CUTTING (e.g. see p. 74), remember that:
1 newspapers can be BIASED in favour of one side or another.
2 newspapers often exaggerate or twist the facts to make a good story.
3 there's quite a difference between a fact and an OPINION: sometimes newspapers report opinions as though they were facts.

So always read the cutting carefully and ask yourself whether it contains FACTS or OPINIONS, or whether it's one-sided.

Each time you look at a PHOTOGRAPH (e.g. see p. 118), look at it carefully. Pictures can often say much more than words. But you should be able to put into words what you see in the picture. What do you think this photograph is 'saying'?

CARTOONS can be fun. They often help you to learn something in an amusing way. What's the message in the cartoons on p. 33?

Each time you come across a table of figures or STATISTICS (e.g. see p. 20) remember that statistics are a mathematical way of giving facts or information.

1 Look at the figures carefully.
2 What does each line of figures or column of figures mean?
3 Make sure you understand the relationship between the different lines and columns.

4 Be able to explain in your own words what the figures mean.
5 What do the figures in this table tell you?

ASKING QUESTIONS

Probably the easiest way of finding things out is by asking someone who is likely to know the answer.
Suppose you want to know:

1 what makes a person become a priest?
2 how many council houses were built in your area last year?
3 what's the most difficult part of being a social worker?

Some questions (e.g. 2) need straightforward factual answers. Others (like 1 and 3) ask for opinions. What should you bear in mind when asking someone for his opinion?

The best person to ask isn't your friend, or even your teacher — unless either of them happens to be a priest, the Director of Housing or a social worker.

1 Whom should you ask?
2 How should you go about it?

WRITING LETTERS

If you can't ask the experts in person, you can write to them instead. A good letter should read something like this:

The Director of Housing,
Coundon District Council,
The Guildhall,
Coundon CV2 1XY

Class 4B,
Lillington Green School,
Stockwell Road,
Coundon, CV4 6JD

18 September 1977

Dear Mr Jacobs,

I am doing an investigation about multi-storey flats as part of my studies at school and I should be very grateful if you could help me. Please could you give me the answers to the following questions?

(a) How many people in Coundon are housed in multi-storey flats?
(b) Does the council have plans to build any more flats in Coundon?
(c) Does the council policy let old age pensioners live in multi-storey flats?
(d) What is the council's policy about families with young children living in multi-storey flats?
(e) What special play facilities are provided inside and outside council multi-storey flats?

I do hope that you can help me and I look forward to receiving your reply.

Yours sincerely,

Bill Smith

Discuss with your teacher why it is important to make your letters neat, precise and polite.

Write a letter to:

1 your MP asking about his/her jobs as an MP.
2 the editor of the local newspaper asking about his/her attitude to censorship.
3 the organizer of a national charity asking how you can help to raise money.

You'll find some useful addresses on p. 160.

LOOKING OUTSIDE

You'll find the answers to the questions in this book in various places. The important thing is to become an expert in knowing where and how to find them out.

VISITING THE LIBRARY

As you work through this book you will be asked to find out all you can about: mods and rockers; trade unions; town planning; how a television programme is made. There will be scores of other topics to choose from too.

In each case a good starting point is to visit the library and to find all the books you can which have information about the topic you've chosen. Ask your teacher or the librarian for help if you're stuck.

As you read through the books, make notes as you go along. They'll help you to remember things later, when you come to write up your account.

NEVER COPY GREAT CHUNKS OUT OF THE BOOKS (unless you're taking down a quotation). Anybody can copy out passages without either understanding or thinking about them at all. You won't learn much in this way.

INTERVIEWS

When you ask someone a series of questions, it's called an INTERVIEW.

Why might some interviews not be very successful?

You've no doubt seen people being interviewed on television. Your job is a bit more difficult because TV interviewers are adults, usually with quite a bit of influence. You're only a school pupil, with very little influence. So remember:

1 Choose a time that's convenient for the people you're interviewing. If they look busy, ask someone else, or come back later.
2 They won't know much about you, and will probably judge you by your manners and appearance. So if you want their help, it's a good idea to be as neat and polite as possible.
3 Explain that you're doing a study for school and that you want to ask them a few questions.
4 When you've finished the interview, thank them for their trouble.

Before you begin, though, you should have decided on the best way of recording what they say. You can use several methods:

a) Remember what they say, and write it down when you get back to school.
b) Write it down while they're speaking.
c) Use a portable tape-recorder, and then write their answers down later, after you've played back the tape.

Discuss together the pros and cons of each of these methods. Which do you think would be the best method and why? (You may find that one method is best in one situation and one in another.)

SURVEYS AND SAMPLES

SURVEYS are a way of finding out:

1 what a number of people think about a certain topic, or
2 how they think they would behave in certain circumstances.

Here are three questions you might ask and some possible answers:

1 Q. If there was a general election tomorrow which political party would you vote for?
   A. Labour. Conservative. Other party. No one.
2 Q. Do you think that men should do as much housework as women?
   A. Yes. No. Don't know.
3 Q. How many times a month do you usually go to the cinema?
   A. Once or less. Twice. Three to four times. More than four times.

In most cases you only want a one-word answer or a short sentence.

Look at question 2. Say you asked thirty people and fifteen said 'yes', six said 'no', and nine said 'don't know'. You could conclude from your survey that fifty percent of the people questioned thought that men should do as much housework as women. Twenty percent thought they shouldn't. And thirty percent didn't know. You may think that thirty people isn't very many to ask. But it would be impossible to ask everyone. You have to ask as many as you think will give you a fair idea of PUBLIC OPINION or public behaviour. The group of people you choose is called a SAMPLE of the population.

There are two main types of samples: a RANDOM SAMPLE and a BALANCED SAMPLE. A random sample is drawn up by picking names out of a hat at random, or by asking the first twenty or thirty people you meet in the street.

In some surveys it's more important to make sure that you have a CROSS-SECTION of the population. In question 2, for example, the result would be affected by whether you asked men or women. So your sample should be BALANCED – half men and half women.

The answer to question 3 might be affected by whether people were young or old. So a balanced sample would include a third young people, a third middle-aged people and a third older people.

The answer to question 1 might be affected by whether people were middle class or working class, men or women, and young or old. In this case a balanced sample would be quite difficult to get. But the more balanced it was, the more reliable your findings would be.

Work out questions, decide on a sample and do surveys to find out:

1 Whether people prefer BBC or ITV news programmes.
2 Which daily newspapers are most popular.
3 Whether or not people agree with corporal punishment in school.

QUESTIONNAIRES

Questionnaires are used when you want to ask several people a number of questions. You can either read out the questions and write their answers in yourself or let them fill in their own answers to a questionnaire you've prepared beforehand.

Questionnaires are one of the best ways of finding out information and are widely used by sociologists. But they're very difficult to produce.

These are the steps to follow:

Step 1   Decide what topic you're going to investigate.
Step 2   Decide what kind of information you need to know.
Step 3   Prepare a questionnaire. (This is the difficult bit!)
Step 4   Decide on a sample and duplicate the necessary number of questionnaires so that people can each have a copy.
         (A number that can be divided by 10 is easiest.)
Step 5   Get the questionnaires filled in.
Step 6   Gather all the information together from all the questionnaires. Total up the answers.
         (Another difficult bit.)
Step 7   Write a report to describe your findings.

Tips to help you with Step 3:

1 Make the questions as short and precise as possible.
2 Don't let you own opinions or prejudice influence the way you ask the questions. Keep them as simple as possible.
3 Don't ask too many questions — people will get fed up answering them.
4 Don't ask questions which people might think are rude or too personal. You'll only annoy them and they won't want to help you.
5 Discuss the questions with your teacher before you try them out on anyone.
6 Try them out on a few friends first to see that there are no problems, and then on your real sample.

Tips to help you with Step 6:

1 You may find it's easiest to use a pocket calculator to add up the answers.
2 If you don't have a calculator, make an 'answer chart' for each question. For example, if you asked the question 'How many hours did you spend watching television last night?' your answer chart would look like this:

			total
A	1 hour or less	✓✓ ✓✓ ✓✓	6
B	1½ - 2 hours	✓✓✓ ✓✓✓ ✓✓✓	9
C	3 - 4 hours	✓✓✓ ✓✓✓ ✓✓✓ ✓✓✓✓	13
D	5 - 6 hours	✓✓✓	3

As you go through the questionnaires, put a tick in column A every time someone answered 1 hour or less, in column B every time someone answered 1½ – 2 hours, and so on. Then count up the ticks.

3 Discuss your findings with your teacher and get his/her advice on the best way of sorting them out.
4 Fill in the questionnaire on page 17 for yourself — just to see what it feels like! Compare your answers with others in the class and add up your replies. What percentage of people in the class
   a) belong to a fan club?
   b) buy pop records?
   c) prefer singles to LPs?
   d) think that pop music should be studied in school?
   e) think that pop stars should earn more than the prime minister?
   f) think that pop stars should earn more than footballers?
5 Who are the three favourite pop stars or groups of people in your class? At what age did most people become interested in pop music? What type of pop music is most popular in your class?

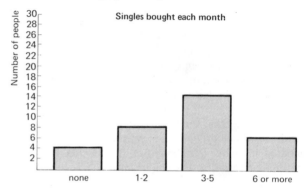

6 Make BAR CHARTS like this to show:
   a) how many singles are bought by people in your class each month.
   b) how many LPs are bought each year.
7 Describe some of the main reasons given in answer to questions 14 and 16 in the questionnaire.
8 Write a report to describe your findings entitled 'Class . . . .'s attitudes to Pop Music'.
9 Try out the questionnaire on a sample of teenagers in a different age group and compare their answers with yours.
      Suppose you wanted to find out what teenagers do in their spare time.
   a) Discuss together what kinds of information you need to know.
   b) Make up a questionnaire designed to give you this information. Discuss the questions together very carefully.
   c) Try it out on a small sample of teenagers.
   d) Total up all the answers.
   e) Write a report to describe your findings. Use bar charts to illustrate some of your findings.

QUESTIONNAIRE ON POP MUSIC

Please fill in the answers to these questions in the space provided,
or tick the answer which applies to you.

1 Age Group:
   11-12
   13-14
   15-16
   17-20

2 Sex:
   Male
   Female

3 Which are your three favourite pop stars or pop groups in
   order of importance?

4 Do you belong to a fan club?   Yes   No

5 If so, which one?

6 At what age did you first become interested in pop music?
   Never
   8 years old or less
   Between 8 and 10 years
   Between 11 and 12 years
   Between 13 and 15 years.

7 Do you buy pop records?
   Yes
   No

8 If Yes, which do you usually buy?
   Singles
   LPs
   An equal number of both singles and LPs

9 How many singles do you buy on average each month?
   None
   2 or less
   Between 3 and 5
   6 or more

10 How many LPs do you buy on average each year?
   None
   2 or less
   Between 3 and 5
   6 or more

11 Which kind of pop music do you prefer
   Rock
   Soul
   Reggae
   Progressive
   Commercial
   No preferences
   Other (Please say which)

12 Do you think that pop music should be studied in school?
   Yes
   No
   Don't know

13 Do you think that pop stars should be paid more than footballers?
   Yes
   No
   Don't know

14 Please give your reasons.

15 Do you think that pop stars should be paid more than the Prime Minister?
   Yes
   No
   Don't know

16 Please give your reasons.

Thank you for answering this questionnaire.

2 FACTS AND FIGURES

Before looking at people's behaviour in society, you need to know a few facts and figures about the people you're studying. The statistics in this chapter will show you how the population of Britain has changed over the last seventy years or so and how it compares with other countries.

1901

1973

37millions

54.3millions

Year	Millions
1901	37.0
1911	40.8
1921	42.7
1931	44.7
1951	48.8
1961	51.4
1971	54.0
1973	54.3

Remember that:

Great Britain means England, Scotland and Wales.
The United Kingdom means England, Scotland, Wales and Northern Ireland.

1 Find out the current size of the population of the following countries:
   United Kingdom, United States, Sweden, Italy, New Zealand, Jamaica, Pakistan, Holland.
2 From a map of the world, write down all the countries which are approximately the same land-size as the UK.
   Compare the size of their population with that of the UK at the present time. What does this tell you?

A good source of population figures for different countries is the *United Nations Yearbook* .

Facts and figures about the population of Great Britain are published each year by Her Majesty's Stationery Office (HMSO) in a book called *Social Trends*. Also useful is *Facts in Focus* (Penguin). You should be able to find these in any good library.

THE CENSUS

On the night of 25 to 26 April 1971, the population in Britain was counted in the latest national CENSUS. A representative from every household of people had to fill in a census form. If they didn't, or if they gave false information, they were fined £50. If they refused to pay the fine they were sent to prison.

Except for 1941, this mammoth operation has taken place every ten years since 1801. The questions on the form have changed over the years. This is the kind of information they provide today:

1 How many people live in Britain. How many are born each year and how many die.
2 Their names, ages, sex and dates of birth.
3 Whether they're single, married, divorced or separated.
4 Details about when they married and how many children they have.
5 Their NATIONALITY and the nationality of their parents.
6 Their educational qualifications and training.
7 What kind of job they do and how many hours a week they work.
8 How many are unemployed or change jobs regularly.
9 Where they work, how they get there and whether they have a car or van for their own use.
10 Whether they rent or own their houses.
11 How many people live in the house.
12 Whether the houses are in good repair with BASIC AMENITIES like hot water, a bathroom and an inside lavatory.

WHY DOES THE GOVERNMENT NEED THIS INFORMATION?

In a society like ours which is always changing the Government needs to plan ahead. It has to know how many and what sorts of people it's planning for.

It needs to know how many schools, houses and roads to build and in what areas. How much money to set aside for health and welfare services. What proportion of the population is either too young or too old to support itself. Which areas have a lot of unemployment and need to have new jobs created.

The details from all the forms are fed into a computer and the information comes out the other end as a collection of statistics. But the forms themselves are kept secret. Sociologists and historians won't be able to inspect the 1971 census forms until the year 2071.

WHY FINES AND IMPRISONMENT?

Why is it necessary to have the threat of fines and imprisonment to make people fill in their forms?

The reason is simple — to make sure everyone does it, especially those who normally 'couldn't be bothered'.

But some people object to filling in the form. They're suspicious of what they call 'Government snooping'. They may have something to hide and they're afraid that the information might be used against them in the future. For example, the form asks personal questions about whether men and women who are living together are married and whether children are legitimate or illegitimate. Immigrants and the children of parents not born in Britain may be afraid that the information they give could be used by an unsympathetic government to expel them from the country.

Others have nothing to hide but they feel that the census is an invasion of their privacy. Why should they be forced to tell government officials personal details about themselves and their family?

Whatever their reasons, though, the law is fairly severe on those who refuse.

IMPORTANCE OF THE CENSUS

Whether or not you agree with the census, it has at least helped us to see how the population has changed since 1801. But we still need to ask why these changes have come about.

1 What is the purpose of the census?
2 Why do some people object to the census?
3 How long must sociologists and historians wait before they are allowed to inspect census forms? Why are they likely to be interested in them?
4 Can you suggest why no national census was taken in 1941?

To find out what the last census discovered you can write to the Census Division, Customer Services Section, Titchfield, Hampshire.

THE BIRTH RATE

Do women have more babies today or fewer than in 1901? Do women in America, India, and Russia have more or fewer babies than women in Britain? To find the answer to questions like these, it's no good just comparing the total number of births in any one year. There would obviously be more in America, India and Russia, because there are more women in these countries to produce the babies.

So to make a fair comparison we have to use a different method, something we call the BIRTH RATE. The Birth Rate takes into account the number of births *and* the size of the existing population.

To calculate the Birth Rate you need to know:
a) the number of births in one year and
b) the size of the existing population in thousands in that same year.

You then *divide* the number of births *by* the number of thousands in the population like this:

$$\frac{\text{Number of births}}{\substack{\text{Number of thousands in} \\ \text{the population}}} = \text{BIRTH RATE}$$

Imagine a town called Ex, with a population of 16 000 people:

In 1973 there were 176 births in town. The Birth Rate for that year therefore was 11.

$$\frac{176}{16} = 11$$

In other words, another 11 people per thousand were added to the population of Ex in 1973.

Birth Rate in Great Britain 1901–1973

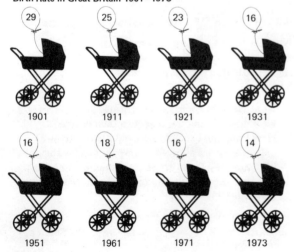

a) How many people per thousand were added to the population of Britain in each of these years?
b) Is the Birth Rate in Great Britain increasing or decreasing?

Each year some of the babies born are illegitimate. The percentage may seem small, but as you can see the figure has almost doubled since the war.

Percentage of Illegitimate Live Births

Year	%	Year	%
1901	4 *	1961	6
1911	5	1971	8
1921	5	1972	8
1931	5	1973	8
1951	5		

* i.e. 4 babies in every 100 born that year were illegitimate.

The proportion of mothers who are pregnant when they get married is quite high, too.

Percentage of Legitimate Live Births Conceived BEFORE marriage

Year	Mother aged under 20	Mother aged 20 – 24
1961	57 +	11
1971	57	10
1972	56	10
1973	56	10

+ i.e. 57 in every 100 girls under 20 years old were pregnant when they got married.

1 Imagine that Zed is a city with a population of 300 000. If there were 4 500 births there in 1975 what would the Birth Rate have been?
2 Draw a graph to show how the Birth Rate in Britain decreased between 1901 and 1973.
3 Using the *United Nations Yearbook,* find out the Birth Rate for the following countries in 1975: United Kingdom, United States, Sweden, Italy, New Zealand, Jamaica, Pakistan, Holland.
4 Make a list of the countries whose Birth Rate is about the same as ours. Make a list of those where the Birth Rate is much higher. What kind of countries seem to have a high Birth Rate? Find out why the Birth Rate is high in these countries.
5 What percentage of births in Britain in 1973 were not illegitimate?
6 How could you turn the figure of eight per cent into the actual number of illegitimate births in 1973?
7 The percentage of babies conceived before marriage has dropped slightly since 1961. Can you suggest any reasons for this?

THE DEATH RATE

The number of people who die each year is also related to the size of the existing population and is expressed in the same way as the Birth Rate. In this case, though, it's called the DEATH RATE.

It is calculated like this:

$$\frac{\text{Total number of deaths}}{\text{Number of thousands in the population}} = \text{DEATH RATE}$$

So in the town of Ex, if 160 people died in 1973, the Death Rate for that year would have been 10.

$$\frac{160}{16} = 10$$

In other words, out of every thousand people living in Ex in 1973, 10 died.

The Death Rate in Great Britain 1901-1973

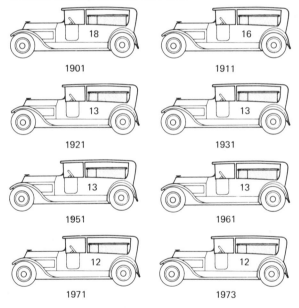

INFANT MORTALITY RATE

If the death occurs within the first year of a baby's life, it's called INFANT MORTALITY. The INFANT MORTALITY RATE for any one year is calculated by dividing the number of infant deaths by the number of thousands of live births.

In 1901 the Infant Mortality Rate in Britain was 185, which meant that for every thousand babies born, 185 died during the first year of life.

By 1973 the Infant Mortality Rate had dropped to 19. That meant that for every thousand babies born, 19 died during the first year of life.

Infant Mortality Rate in Great Britain 1901–1973

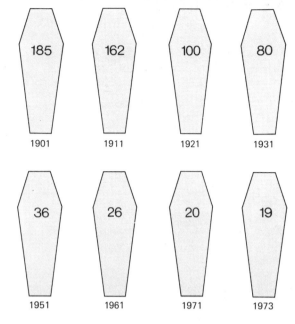

1 If the Death Rate for the city of Zed (pop. 300 000) in 1975 was 13, what was the actual number of deaths in the city that year?

2 Make a list of the countries where the Death Rate is about the same as ours. Make a list of the countries where the Death Rate is much higher. What kind of countries seem to have a high Death Rate? Find out why the Death Rate is high in these countries.

3 By comparing the Birth and Death Rates of Britain in 1901, 1931, and 1971, how could you find out the rate of population increase in those years?

4 Make a list of the countries in which the Infant Mortality Rate is still very high. Explain why the Infant Mortality Rate is high in these countries.

5 Draw a graph to show the reduction in the Infant Mortality Rate in Britain between 1901 and 1973.

6 Suggest reasons why the Infant Mortality Rate has been dramatically reduced during the last seventy years, then do some research from history books in the library to see if you're right. What other reasons can you find in the books apart from your own?

7 The changes in the Infant Mortality Rate have been much more dramatic than the changes in the Death Rate. Can you suggest why?

8 Although the Birth Rate declined between 1901 and 1973, the size of the population increased. Can you explain why?

LIFE EXPECTANCY

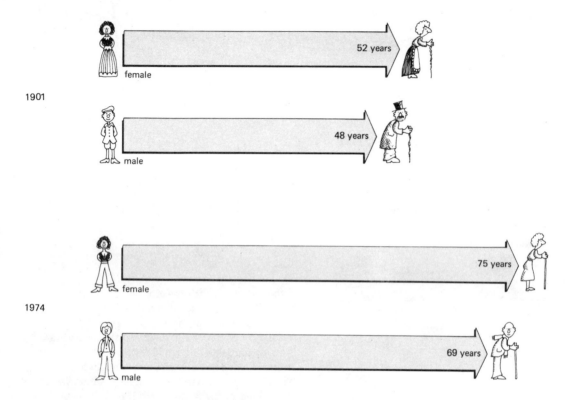

1901

female — 52 years

male — 48 years

1974

female — 75 years

male — 69 years

Not only do more babies survive these days, but they can expect to live much longer too. And if the babies are girls, they're even more likely than boys to reach a 'ripe old age'. Look at the differences for babies born in 1901 and 1974.

1 Do these figures mean that all the girls born in 1901 died at fifty-two years of age and all the boys died at forty-eight? Explain your answer carefully.

2 Suggest reasons why
   a) women tend to live longer than men.
   b) the *expectation of life* has increased by an average of twenty years in the last seventy years.

   Now do some research from history books to see if you're right. What other reasons can you find in the books apart from your own?

3 Find out the life expectancy today for men and women in the following countries:
   Sweden, Italy, New Zealand, United States, Jamaica, Holland, Pakistan.

4 Make a list of the countries in which the expectation of life is much shorter than in Britain. Why is the expectation of life shorter in these countries?

FAMILY AND MARRIAGE

Average Age of Men and Women at First Marriage

Year	1901	1911	1921	1931	1951	1961	1971
Men	27.2	27.3	27.6	27.4	26.8	25.6	24.6
Women	25.6	25.6	25.5	25.5	24.2	23.3	22.6

Average family size in 1890 and . . .

now.

1 Suggest reasons why women tend to marry younger than men.
2 Suggest as many reasons as you can why people are marrying younger these days.
3 a) Using *Social Trends*, find out what percentage of the men and women who married last year were under twenty.
   b) Find out what percentage of the men and women who married in 1951 were under twenty.
   c) Has the number of teenage marriages increased, decreased or stayed much the same?

THE ELDERLY

The fact that people live longer today also means that the number of elderly people in the population is growing. If we define elderly as all those men over 65 and all those women over 60, then the numbers increased from 2.9 millions in 1911 to 8.9 millions in 1971.

Here are the actual figures:

Elderly Population in Thousands

	1911	1931	1951	1971
elderly men aged 65 and over	964	1470	2251	2757
elderly women aged 60 and over	1915	2950	4599	6141
total elderly	2879	4420	6850	8890
elderly as a percentage of the total population	6.8%	9.6%	13.6%	16.0%

From studying the census figures carefully the experts have been able to forecast that in the next twenty years or so the number of elderly people in the population will increase and they will also live longer.

Forecast for 2001:

Total number of elderly in the population

9½ millions

36.3% of elderly men will be over 75

37.6% of elderly women will be over 75

1 Why is the definition of an elderly person different for a man and a woman?

2 Why has the percentage of elderly people in the population increased since 1911?

3 People who are over the age of retirement are given pensions by the State. The money to pay for Old Age Pensions comes partly from the taxes paid by people who are working and partly from NATIONAL INSURANCE CONTRIBUTIONS. What will have to happen in the next twenty years if - as the experts forecast - the number of elderly people is going to increase faster than the number of people going out to work?

THE CHANGING PATTERN OF LIFE

If we put all this information together and add a few other details about the age at which people usually leave school, start work, get married and have children, we can see just how much the pattern of people's lives has changed since the beginning of the century. The difference is most striking for women.

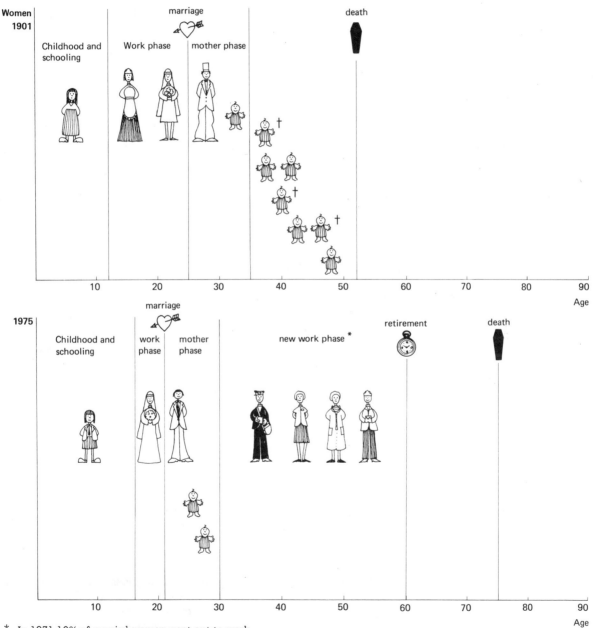

* In 1931 10% of married women went out to work.
  In 1971 40% of married women went out to work.

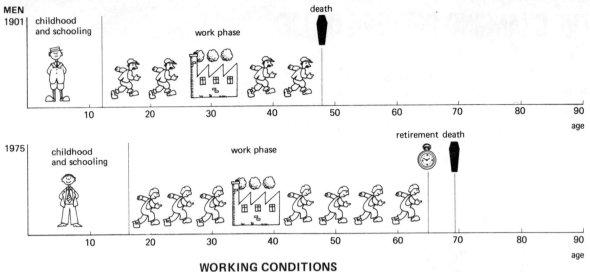

WORKING CONDITIONS

Although people now spend longer in full-time employment, wages and conditions have steadily improved. During the last twenty years, for example, the average number of hours worked each week has decreased and the average number of holidays each year (usually with pay) has increased.

AVERAGE WORKING WEEK

1951   1973

WORKERS' HOLIDAYS

	1951		1975	
up to 1 week		28%		0%
1 to 2 weeks		69%		6%
2 to 3 weeks		3%		9%
3 weeks or more		0%		85%

1 How long did the average woman spend in childbirth and child-rearing in 1901? in 1975?
2 Suggest reasons why people are having fewer children today than seventy years ago.
3 What was the average age of marriage for women in 1901 and 1975?
4 What has been the main change in women's working lives outside the home during the last seventy years?
5 What has happened to women's life expectancy during the last seventy years?
6 Explain how the pattern of men's lives has changed during the last twenty years.
7 In what ways have working conditions improved during the last twenty years? Find out the average number of hours worked each week by men and women in 1901 and 1931.*
8 Find out the average weekly wage for working men and women in 1901, 1931, 1951, 1975 and the present day.*
9 Conduct a small survey to find out the average number of weeks' holiday per year for fathers of pupils in your class.

*You will find *Social Trends* helpful in answering these questions.

Ration children two by two, warns Professor 'Noah'

If you think 1984 is going to be bad, don't hang around until 2010.

That is the year when, according to the experts, the world population will have doubled.

The year when the birth rate could be controlled by 'child coupons' and couples who have had more than two children could be punished in their old age for 'anti-social' behaviour.

These are not the products of the current vogue for Doomwatch fiction. They are presented as real possibilities by gynaecologist and population expert Professor Derek Llewellyn-Jones.

The problem, he says, is that men and women will insist on going forth and multiplying.

Only hope

When one and one make two children, it's all right — but when one and one make three or four or more, it brings the doomsters out in a rash of statistics.

For instance, by the first year of the Christian era the world's population was 250 million and it took another 1,650 years to double it. But this year the world population is 4,000 million — and it will take only another 35 years for it to double.

Professor Llewellyn-Jones, a Briton who works at the University of Sydney, believes man's only hope is to balance the books: 'To change our attitude so that we reach a state of global equilibrium, in which births and deaths are equal.'

We will know within our own lifetimes whether the world will pull through, whether it makes the right choices. But, says the professor in Old Testament tones: 'If the solutions are wrong, or fail to work, a disaster of unprecedented magnitude will sweep the earth, and neither adults nor their children will be spared.'

The key is the two-child family. If most couples could 'contain their urge for procreation' and restrict themselves to two children, population replacement level would be achieved.

Couples who had more than two children would be penalised. Only those restricting their families would receive full old-age pensions; the 'anti-social' couples would have their pensions reduced and be dependent on their 'extra' children to make it up.

Every 15-year-old girl would be issued with 20 child coupons and give up 10 after each birth. Childless women could sell their coupons to families wanting more than two children

An unmarried mother who did not wish to keep her child would surrender 10 coupons and get them back from the mother who adopts her child.

How can a highly-trained, much-respected mind come up with these ideas?

'I am neither a gloomy prophet of doom nor am I an optimistic technological ostrich,' insists the author of *People Populating*.'I am Noah's man.'

The twentieth-century Noah will build his ark 'by controlling his birth rate, by adopting a new ecologically sane technology, and by replacing greed with gratitude'.

The prophetic professor does not mention another school of thought which reckons man's common sense — plus a little help from above — will see us through. And that if he succeeds in his doomster plans to curtail liberties and put a price on human life, the world wouldn't be worth saving anyway.

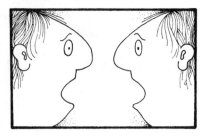

Discuss together with your teacher any of the words in the cutting which you don't understand.

What is Professor Llewellyn-Jones' idea for the future? Do you think the reporter agrees with him?

Suggest as many points as you can for and against the Professor's views.

When you've considered both sides of the argument, make a speech giving your own opinion and your reasons for either supporting or rejecting Professor Llewellyn-Jones' ideas.

Using the information from the charts, fill in the correct answers in the spaces below:

1 The population of Great Britain increased by _____ millions between 1901 and 1973.

2 To calculate the birth rate you divide _____ by _____ .

3 The birth rate in Britain dropped from _____ to _____ between 1901 and 1973.

4 The infant mortality rate is calculated by dividing _____ by _____ .

5 The infant mortality rate in 1901 was nearly _____ times higher than in 1973.

6 The average expectation of life for girls born in 1974 was _____ years.

7 The average expectation of life for boys has increased from _____ years to _____ years between 1901 and 1974.

8 In 2001 the experts forecast that _____ of elderly men and _____ of elderly women will be over seventy-five.

9 In 1975 the average number of hours worked each week was _____ .

10 In 1975 _____ % of workers had three or more weeks' holiday with pay.

1

Make a scrap-book to illustrate 'The Changing Lives of Men and Women in the Twentieth Century' with one chapter for each decade.

Try to show as many aspects of life as you can, e.g. clothes, working conditions, family life, leisure activities, transport, wealth and poverty, the effects of war, new inventions etc.

Ask parents and grandparents to help. They may have a useful collection of old photographs, newspapers and souvenirs.

2

Make a study of the work of Oxfam in poor countries with large populations.

3

Make a study of the health of people in Britain during the last hundred years. How have medical knowledge and the Health Service improved? What are the main problems facing the National Health Service today?

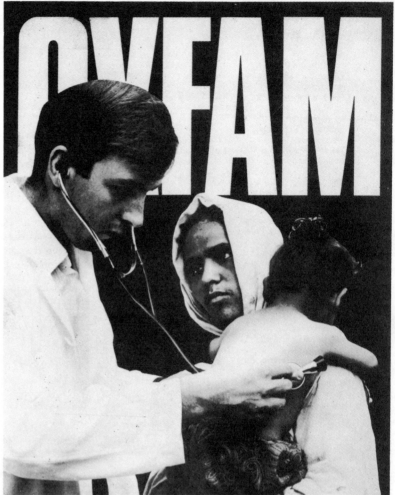

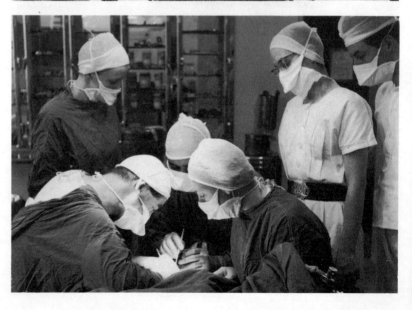

4

Collect the population facts and figures for your village, town or city for last year. Produce colourful and clear charts to show the number of births, marriages and deaths, and what proportion of the population was male, female, below school age, of school age and elderly. Write for information to the local Registrar or County Planning Office.

5

Choose one country said to be experiencing a 'population explosion'. Describe exactly what this means, what problems are involved and what needs to be done to help solve them. Write for information to Oxfam or Christian Aid.

6

Make a guide for elderly people in your area about social activities and clubs run for their benefit. Add a list of shops, hairdressers, cinemas, etc., where they are entitled to specially reduced prices. Include information about local authority and voluntary services designed to help old people from the local information office or the Citizens' Advice Bureau.

3 CHILDHOOD

Childhood is a very important time in the life of human beings, important because children grow and develop more in their first few years of life than at any other time later on.

At two and a half this little girl has already reached half her full adult height.

These eight-year-olds already know half the words they will ever use as adults.

This boy and girl are already playing at jobs which will be expected of them by our society when they grow up.

NATURE OR NURTURE

Two things affect the way children behave and the kind of people they become.

NATURE — or the intelligence and talents they are born with and which they inherit in their biological make-up from their parents

and

NURTURE — or the ways in which they are brought up, and the things and people around them who influence them.

No one can say for certain which is most important, nature or nurture. But because so much growth takes place in the first few years of life, it's important to find out how much this is influenced by the child's earliest experiences in the world.

In studying childhood, therefore, it's necessary to look at children in relation to
a) the family which brings them up
b) the neighbourhood they grow up in
c) the society they live in

If you'd been taken — a few days after you were born — to live with a different family in a different society, you'd be a very different sort of person by now. If you'd been brought up by Eskimos or Chinese peasants, Bushmen of the Kalahari Desert or American Indians, your whole personality and way of life would have been influenced by their customs, beliefs and traditions.

You'd have spoken their language, dressed in their fashions, and learned the behaviour expected by their society. Even if you'd been brought up by a different family in another part of the country, this would have changed the sort of person you are.

Let's take an extreme example.

Imagine that like Charles and Anne in this photo you'd been brought up in the royal family. Make notes on how your life would have been different, using the following headings:
house, neighbourhood, clothes, wealth, education, holidays and travel, hobbies and leisure activities, pets, meeting people, boy/girl friends, ambitions for the future.

Three children whose upbringing has obviously affected the kind of people they have become.

CHILDREN'S NEEDS

All children need to be looked after until they are old enough and experienced enough to take care of themselves. At birth a new-born baby is almost completely helpless. He/she needs the care and protection of someone older. In most cases (though not all) this means the child's parents and family.

But families differ. Some are large, some small. Some are wealthy, others are not so wealthy. Some live in expensive houses in pleasant neighbourhoods, others are homeless. Some are loving and happy, others experience the kind of problems which may lead to arguments and separation. In between each extreme are hundreds of families, each of them with their own particular characteristics. And all of these characteristics have an influence on the growing child.

Here are some of the things which experts believe good parents should provide for children growing up. Can you add any others of your own?

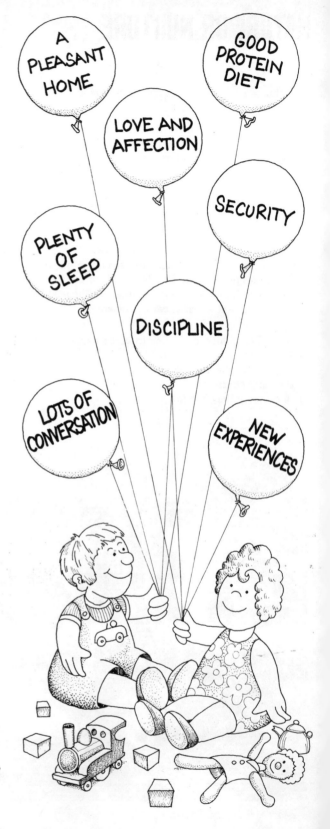

1 Discuss together with your teacher what each of these things means and why it is important. Why is it necessary to the child now? How will it help him/her in the future?

2 Sometimes, through no fault of their own, parents are unable to provide all of these things for their children. What circumstances or reasons might prevent families from providing these things? Explain each one as fully as you can.

3 Sometimes parents neglect or harm their children because they have problems themselves. Give examples, if you can, from your own knowledge or experience of cases in which parents either injured or neglected their children when they themselves were in some kind of trouble.

4 For some parents, there's no excuse for their behaviour. They neglect or injure their children through thoughtlessness and ignorance. Give examples from your own knowledge or experience of parents who you think are to blame in this way. Are you sure that your criticisms are fair? What evidence have you to support your opinions?

5 Some parents 'spoil' their children.
   a) Give examples from your own knowledge or experience of the kind of things that parents do which 'spoil' children.
   b) What effects does this have on the children now?
   c) What effects might this have on the children in the future?

LEARNING SEX ROLES

Childhood is the time when children begin to learn that boys and girls are different, and that our society expects males and females to do different things and behave in different ways.

   Probably the first thing that's ever said about a new-born baby is 'It's a boy' or 'It's a girl'. And from that moment on, society begins to teach it the behaviour and attitudes that go with its sex.

   We'll see in later chapters how this is done at school and in adult life, but the first lessons in learning how to be masculine and feminine come from parents and experiences in childhood.

Quite often boys and girls are dressed differently.

Adults often use different words about boys and girls.

Sometimes parents expect different behaviour from boys and girls.

Girls are often encouraged to copy their mothers and boys to imitate their fathers. Sometimes they're given toys with which they can pretend to be like Mum or Dad.

*Look back to p. 8 for information about roles.

In their games children often imitate what they see men and women in society doing.

1 Children's fashions have changed in recent years, and like adults, both sexes seem to wear jeans these days. But show by pictures, drawings and descriptions how you can still tell the difference between boys and girls by their dress and appearance.

2 Ask some parents of young babies the questions, 'You have a little girl. Would you mind if people kept thinking she was a boy?' 'You have a little boy. Would you mind if people kept thinking he was a girl?' Ask them to give reasons for their answers.

3 What different attitudes to boys and girls are hidden behind the words 'pretty' and 'strong' in the drawings on page 33?
Make a list of other words which are:
a) usually used about girls.
b) usually used about boys.
c) used for either sex.
d) Explain what kind of picture of boys and girls these lists of words conjure up in your mind.

4 a) Give examples of things, besides those shown on page 33, that girls are supposed to do and not supposed to do to become 'nice young ladies'.
b) Give examples of things boys are supposed to do and not supposed to do to become 'real men'.

5 But some girls do fight and act like tomboys. Some boys do cry and like playing with dolls.

From your own knowledge or experience say whether parents, friends and relatives accept this behaviour without question or whether they try to encourage the children to behave in 'a more appropriate way'. Give examples to illustrate your answer.

6 Observe a group of children playing in someone's garden, in a play-group, in the street where you live, or in a playground. Make detailed notes in turn about boys, girls, and both sexes with
a) their toys.
b) the games they play.
c) the outfits and uniforms (e.g. cowboy outfit, nurse's uniform) they wear.
d) Write a paragraph to describe your observations explaining to what extent the children's toys and games are helping them to learn their sex roles.

7 Here are some questions to think about and discuss together:
a) Why shouldn't boys learn to cook and clean up the house?
b) Why shouldn't girls learn about cars and machinery and how to use tools?
c) Why shouldn't girls play football?
d) Why shouldn't boys play with dolls?
e) What are the advantages and disadvantages of boys and girls learning different sex roles?

CHILDREN'S READERS

John and Mary are a brother and sister of about the same age. They live in a trouble-free world where the sun is always shining and people are always smiling. They have a nice house where the flowers and rolling lawns seem to grow of their own accord. Unlike most children, John and Mary are never cold, hungry, bad-tempered, misbehaved or bored. They rarely quarrel and Mummy and Daddy never say 'No'.

For the children in reading books and their parents life has no problems and no conflicts. They also play very definite sex roles. Look at the picture here. Mummy is hardly ever seen outside the kitchen except to help the children tidy their toys, feed them, put them to bed and wake them up in the morning. Her life is routine and domestic. She doesn't go out to work. She doesn't even drive the car. Mary is encouraged to copy her. 'Mary has to help Mummy work in the house.' 'Mary wants to make cakes like Mummy.'

Daddy drives the car, paints the house, teaches John to make boats and airplanes and always leads the children in their most interesting activities. He never helps in the kitchen. He is always looked after by Mummy.

John helps Daddy with the car, in the garden and painting the house. His games are always exciting — flying an airplane, making a boat, boxing, underwater swimming, playing doctors or cowboys. Mary frequently stands by, watching admiringly. But her games — drawing, arranging flowers, doing jigsaws, nursing her doll — need much less energy. She mustn't be a tomboy or risk crumpling her dress.

Make a collection of some of the reading books used in primary schools to teach reading (e.g. Ladybird, Janet and John, Happy Venture, Nippers).

1   Is it true that 'the reading-book world is too-good-to-be-true'? Find as many examples as you can to support the claim.
2   Find examples of books which show more 'life-like' children and parents. What makes them more true to life?
3   Does it make any difference whether or not the children, parents and surroundings shown in the books are true to life?
    Give full reasons for your answer.
4   Write a description of a typical reading book Mum and Dad, where they live and how they spend their time. Use quotes and pictures from the books to help you. Now write a description of your own Mum and Dad. In what ways are they the same as those in the books? In what ways different?
5   Make a list of the toys of boys and girls in the books. Do they ever play with the same toys?
6   Make a chart like this to compare the games and activities of the children in the books. Each time you find an example of one of the games or activities described in the chart, put a tick to show whether it's being done by boys or girls.

Types of Games and Activities	Boys	Girls
Games involving action and energy.		
Games involving sitting quietly.		
Activities where one child is taking the lead; who is the leader?		
Games involving caring for other people.		
Games involving being big and strong.		

Add up the number of ticks you have given for boys and girls in each case.

Write a paragraph to describe the difference between boys' and girls' activities in children's reading books.

7   Many teachers are critical of, children's reading books for being 'too-good-to-be-true' and 'too sex-role biased'. Why should these things worry teachers? From your own study, do you agree or disagree with their view?

NSPCC

These examples are from the casefile of the National Society for the Prevention of Cruelty to Children.

A three-week-old baby had been left alone crying piteously. Neighbours telephoned the local Inspector who arrived in time to prevent the baby being suffocated by a sheet.

A three-year-old was found wandering late at night on a busy main road. He was bare-footed and dirty. He had been left alone in the house for hours and had gone in search of his mother. She was eventually traced by the NSPCC.

Children Found Covered in Filth

Four small children left alone in their home by their parents were found soaked in urine covered in white paint. One had excreta on her face and the youngest, a three-month-old baby, was 'Bright blue and frozen'. The NSPCC Inspector, a woman police officer and a social worker agreed that the children's condition was the worst they'd ever seen. In court the mother said that she'd left home after a fight with her husband over money three days before the children were found. 'My husband was only giving me between three and five pounds a week for food,' she said. 'I was scared to go back to the flat because of what my husband might do to me. We had a fight and I told my husband to leave. He wouldn't, so I did. I didn't think he would leave the children on their own.'

The father admitted he only gave his wife five pounds for food, but said he brought food home at weekends. His take-home pay was forty-five pounds.

The children were taken into the care of the local authority.

Alice is six. She's terrified of the dark, loud noises, caterpillars. And her parents.

A woman wrote to the NSPCC 'I dearly love my son and am now petrified to have him around in case I lash out, if not at him, at my daughter who is eight months old. I can't carry on much longer.'

Assaulted by Her Father

Carol agreed to baby-sit for her younger brothers and sisters while her mother played bingo and as a result was assaulted by her father, who banged her head against a chair and kicked her. A doctor who examined the child telephoned the NSPCC when he found extensive bruising on her arm, thigh and behind her ear.

Legal proceedings were taken by the Society and in court the girl's father admitted assaulting his daughter in a way likely to cause unnecessary suffering and injury to health. In a statement he said that he had told his wife not to go out to play bingo when he went to a football match. Nevertheless she did go out, leaving Carol in charge of three younger children aged five, seven and eleven. He was furious with his wife and had apparently taken it out on his daughter.

He was imprisoned for six months.

For his sixth birthday, David's father gave him a belt. Across the face.

Managing Director and His Wife Prosecuted for Neglecting their Child.

In some ways Justin Roberts is a lucky boy. He lives in a large, expensive house. His father is the managing director of a small but prosperous business. His mother is young and attractive. He has all the toys and games a child could want. But he is an unhappy child and last week his parents were prosecuted for neglecting him. On three different occasions the Roberts' cleaning woman let herself into the house to begin work and found Justin alone and crying. When she commented on this to Mrs Roberts, she was told to mind her own business or find other employment. She reported the case to the NSPCC. An Inspector discovered that Mrs Roberts regularly left Justin alone, playing with his toys, whilst she went out to lunch or to see friends. He was two years old.

When Mary spilt her tea, her parents locked her in her room. She was still there when we found her three months later.

The NSPCC helps nearly 200 children a day.

Over forty per cent of the children are under five.

Sometimes parents neglect or harm their children because they have troubles themselves and they don't know where to turn. The NSPCC tries to help parents sort out their troubles so that they can look after their children properly.

The children helped by the NSPCC come from all types of families and all types of background.

Playgroups for children below school age are now being run by the NSPCC in some areas. While the children are being looked after their mothers meet to discuss their problems and difficulties with a trained social worker. The aim is to help mothers cope before they are driven by despair into attacks on their children.

The headquarters of the NSPCC is in London. You can write to them at 1, Riding House Street, London W1P 8AA. There are also many local branches.

1   When was the NSPCC founded and what kind of work does the Society do today?
2   Why was an American girl, Mary Ellen, important in the history of the NSPCC?
3   Ask your teacher to arrange for an NSPCC Inspector to come and tell you about his/her job.
4   What is the difference between parents 'providing proper discipline' for their children and causing them 'unnecessary suffering'?
5   Find out what legal action can be taken against parents convicted of cruelty to children.
6   The NSPCC often relies on people reporting neighbours they suspect of mistreating their children. Discuss together

   a) what kind of evidence and information you would need before you reported parents to the NSPCC
   b) whether or not you have any right to interfere.
   c) whether or not the NSPCC has any right to interfere.

BORN TO FAIL

All the children who were born during the week of 3 – 9 March, 1958 are being studied by the National Children's Bureau. There are 16 000 of them. They come from every corner of Britain, they are fit and handicapped, privileged and deprived, talented and retarded. Information has been collected from a host of experts — doctors, teachers, health-visitors, midwives. We know about their health, their educational progress, their families, homes and schools. In 1969 the children were eleven years old.

NATIONAL CHILD DEVELOPMENT STUDY
Families
One child in every sixteen children in Britain was living with one parent, not two. One child in six lived in a family where there were five children or more. *(Overall the number of eleven-year-olds in either one-parent or large families was one in four).*

Low Income
One child in seven either received free school meals because their parents' wages were very low,or their parents received SUPPLEMENTARY BENEFITS (extra income) from the State because they earned so little.

Poor Housing
One child in six was found to be living in overcrowded conditions (more than one and a half people per room). One child in eleven lived in a home without hot water — which usually meant no bathroom or inside toilet either. *(Overall the number of eleven-year-olds in poor housing was one in four children.)*

SOCIALLY DISADVANTAGED
Some children found themselves in more than one category. Those who were in all three were described as SOCIALLY DISADVANTAGED. One child in sixteen was socially disadvantaged. That meant an average of two children in every class of eleven-year-olds in the country.

REGIONAL DIFFERENCES
Whilst the number of disadvantaged children was one in sixteen over the country as a whole there were regional differences, e.g. :

Southern England	one in forty-seven
Northern England	one in twelve
Wales	one in twelve
Scotland	one in ten

ORDINARY CHILDREN
Those children who did not fit into any category were called ordinary children and made up 63.9% of the total as this diagram shows.

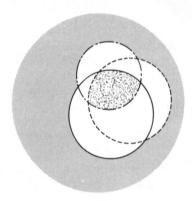

low income family 14.3%   disadvantaged 6.2%

bad housing 22.7%   ordinary (none of these) 63.9%

one parent or large family 23.0%

WHAT DISADVANTAGE MEANS TO CHILDREN

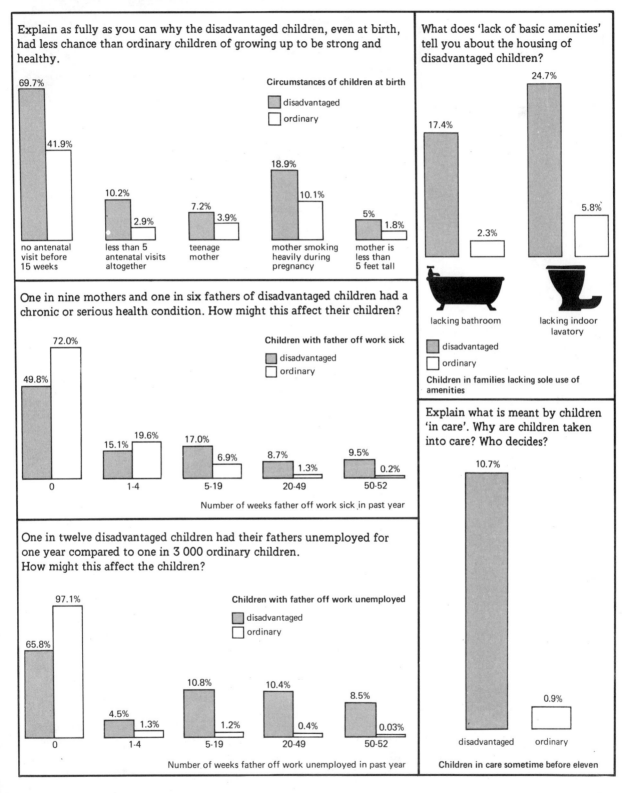

Explain as fully as you can why the disadvantaged children, even at birth, had less chance than ordinary children of growing up to be strong and healthy.

Circumstances of children at birth
- disadvantaged
- ordinary

69.7% / 41.9% no antenatal visit before 15 weeks
10.2% / 2.9% less than 5 antenatal visits altogether
7.2% / 3.9% teenage mother
18.9% / 10.1% mother smoking heavily during pregnancy
5% / 1.8% mother is less than 5 feet tall

What does 'lack of basic amenities' tell you about the housing of disadvantaged children?

17.4% / 2.3% lacking bathroom
24.7% / 5.8% lacking indoor lavatory

- disadvantaged
- ordinary

Children in families lacking sole use of amenities

One in nine mothers and one in six fathers of disadvantaged children had a chronic or serious health condition. How might this affect their children?

Children with father off work sick
- disadvantaged
- ordinary

49.8% / 72.0% — 0
15.1% / 19.6% — 1-4
17.0% / 6.9% — 5-19
8.7% / 1.3% — 20-49
9.5% / 0.2% — 50-52

Number of weeks father off work sick in past year

Explain what is meant by children 'in care'. Why are children taken into care? Who decides?

10.7% disadvantaged / 0.9% ordinary

Children in care sometime before eleven

One in twelve disadvantaged children had their fathers unemployed for one year compared to one in 3 000 ordinary children. How might this affect the children?

Children with father off work unemployed
- disadvantaged
- ordinary

65.8% / 97.1% — 0
4.5% / 1.3% — 1-4
10.8% / 1.2% — 5-19
10.4% / 0.4% — 20-49
8.5% / 0.03% — 50-52

Number of weeks father off work unemployed in past year

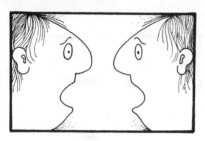

Children between the ages of five and twelve watch more television than any other age-group — about twenty-five hours a week on average.

These two accounts from the local paper are often used as evidence that television is bad for children.

TV Times the Only Book Around

Primary school headmaster Mr Peter Short said today that television is the major cause of poor reading ability among children in his school. 'The television is either on or switched on as soon as they get in from school and it's still on when they go to bed,' he said. 'Mothers don't read stories to children any more. And they seem even less willing to encourage their children to practise reading. The only 'book' in most of the homes round here is the *TV Times*.'

Boy of Ten is a TV Crook

Professional burglars are getting younger every day. A boy of ten admitted to policemen that he got his ideas about house-breaking from TV programmes. He watched burglars on the television and then tried out the techniques for himself. He pleaded guilty to stealing £10 in cash and fifty cigarettes from a house in Russell Street and asked for twelve other cases to be taken into account.

1

Make a study of the TV viewing habits of young children. Try to question as many children as possible. Perhaps a local primary school will help.

1 Find out how many hours a week on average they watch TV and which programmes they prefer.
2 Find out whether children watch programmes which you consider to be violent or which include a lot of sex or swearing.
3 Ask their teachers or parents whether they think that TV viewing helps or hinders the children's education.
4 Do you think adults are more or less likely to be influenced by TV than children? Be able to give good reasons for your opinions.

When you've collected some evidence and some opinions, make a speech to the rest of the class supporting or attacking the view that, 'Children shouldn't be allowed to watch television until they are old enough NOT to be influenced by it'.

2

LATCH-KEY CHILDREN

Latch-key children are those who come home at night to an empty house, empty because their mothers are out at work.

Almost half the women in Britain today are employed in either full-time or part-time work. Of these about sixty-five percent are married women. Most of them have children.

Do you think that the children of working mothers are neglected and likely to get into trouble? Or are they likely to be more independent and self-reliant than children whose mothers don't work? How much depends on the age of the children and the arrangements made by their mothers for some-one to keep an eye on them?

3

WOMEN'S LIB BABY

Helen Gordon is a career girl 1970s style. She has a good job, is well paid and enjoys her life immensely. She has her own house and car and likes the freedom to travel abroad when the mood takes her. But she's strongly opposed to marriage. 'It's a real trap for women,' she says. 'It's always the husband's career that comes first. Wives soon become their unpaid cooks and cleaners. I don't want to be tied down to one man and one house for the rest of my life.'

But Helen likes children and has decided to have one. Do you agree or disagree with her decision? Is she capable of bringing up the child on her own? What about the father? Has he any rights in the matter? What about the baby? Is the love and security of one parent enough? Give as many reasons as you can to support your views.

1 At what age do most children reach half their adult height?
2 Explain the difference between the terms 'nature' and 'nurture'.
3 Which three things most influence the way in which children grow up to be adults?
4 Why does a new-born baby need the care and protection of someone older?
5 Describe three of the ways in which young children begin to learn their sex roles.
6 What do the initials NSPCC stand for?
7 In their Child Development Study, how did the National Children's Bureau define 'socially disadvantaged' children?
8 Which area of Britain has one of the largest proportions of 'socially disadvantaged' children? Can you suggest why?
9 How many hours a week on average do children spend watching television?
10 What is meant by the term 'latch-key' children'?

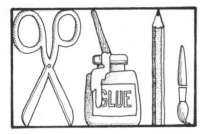

1

Make a scrap-book of a year in the life of a child you know well. Describe with the help of photos how he/she learns through new experiences.

2

'Walking about the street with my hands in my pockets, nobody really cares about me. My only true friend is the black suit I always wear, which I've had for years. People walk about in groups, all gay and laughing, while me, I walk all alone in my old black suit. Suddenly I see someone coming to me, a bunch of boys and girls. How happy I feel. Then they all disappear again and leave me lonely.'

    (from *The Forsaken Lover*,
      by Chris Searle)

Write a story or poem of your own about an only child who feels lonely. Try to get inside the skin of the child. Why is he/she lonely? Try to describe as accurately as you can what it feels like to be lonely.

3

Make a study of children's comics. What are the main differences between those for boys and girls? Use pictures and quotations from the comics to illustrate your project.

4

Yvonne is a thalidomide child. The dangerous drug thalidomide was prescribed to Yvonne's mother and a number of other women during pregnancy. It meant that their children were born with severe physical handicaps. Make a study of handicapped children and find out what can be done to help them live as normal a life as possible.

5

'Jim and Pat live on the sixth floor of a big block of flats in Leeds. Their Dad is a bus driver and their Mum works part-time at Woolworths. Their best friend is called Winston. He lives on the floor below with his mother and two sisters. . .'

Finish off this story for children of eight or nine. Add some pictures to illustrate it. Try to make the characters as true to life as possible. But to be interesting to children, the story must also be exciting. What kind of adventures could Jim and Pat and Winston get up to? When you've finished, try telling the story to some children. The text will need to be simple, the pictures colourful and bright.

6

Punch and Judy are traditional favourites with young children. Make some puppets of your own, write a script and see whether you can take your show into local playgrounds, nurseries, primary schools or children's hospitals.

4 SCHOOL

I would like to say that I enjoyed school today.

We have a nice new building.

My parents bought me a uniform.

The headteacher wanted to be friendly.

The teachers tried to make their lessons interesting.

We had fish and chips for school dinner.

I would like to say that I enjoyed school today.

But I didn't.

Perhaps like 'young Fred' you don't enjoy school very much. Or maybe you think that schools 'exist for your benefit' and have a duty to educate you.

In some poor countries large sections of the population receive little or no schooling. They look enviously at countries like ours where education is compulsory. But do 'education' and 'schooling' necessarily go together? For eleven years of your life, for 200 days every year, you must receive an 'efficient' and 'full-time' education. But the law says nothing about spending that time in school.

There's nothing to stop parents educating their sons and daughters at home, or anywhere else they choose, so long as the education they provide is as good as that given in schools. If it's not, they're breaking the law.

IS THERE A LAW AGAINST IT ?

Test your general knowledge of the laws on schooling and then check your answers by turning to p. 49.

1 Do parents have the right to see teachers about their children's progress?
2 Can headteachers insist that pupils wear school uniform?
3 Can parents complain about detentions?
4 Can teachers confiscate pupils' property?
5 Does the law allow headteachers to cane pupils?
6 Can parents complain about corporal punishment?
7 Do schools have the right to set homework?
8 Can pupils decide themselves what exams to take?
9 Do headteachers have the right to punish pupils for bad behaviour outside school?
10 Which is the only lesson the law insists should be taught in school?

SCHOOLS THEN...

Schools have changed a lot during the last hundred years. You might not think so if you go to a school built before the First World War which looks as though it was designed for a prison! A hundred years ago it was thought enough for most children to be able to read, write and do arithmetic. Discipline was very harsh and pupils were taught to fear and respect their teachers by the frequent use of the cane. Lessons were dull. The aim was to cram into pupils' minds as many facts as possible by making them repeat over and over again the words of the teacher. One reason for this was the size of the classes — sixty pupils to one teacher was quite common. Another reason was to train loyal and hard-working citizens.

The classroom of an elementary school in 1908.

... AND NOW

In 1880 school attendance was made compulsory but parents had to pay between two and eight old pennies a week in fees. This did not please the factory owners who had become used to employing children in the nineteenth century for half the wages paid to adults. Parents also complained that they'd rather have their children earning than learning. So a 'half-time system' was introduced in 1893 which meant that children of ten or eleven could leave school for half-time employment.

The effect on the youngsters was terrible. Ben Turner remembers the day he was ten . . .

'The day I was ten years of age, I went into the mill as a half-timer. We had to go to school one half day and the mill the other half day. One week we started work at 6 a.m. and went on to 12.30 p.m. with a half hour for breakfast. We then had to go to school from 2 until 4.30 p.m. The opposite week we went to school at 9 a.m. until 12 noon, and to work from 1.30 p.m. until 6 p.m. It was a bit cruel at times when on the morning turn at the mill — for it meant being up at 5 a.m., getting a drop of something warm, and trudging off to the mill a mile away to begin work. In winter it was fearful.'

This system continued until 1918 when the school-leaving age was raised to fourteen, but even as late as 1936 the main argument against raising it any further was that children were needed in the factories or on the land.

Many of the children were very poor. Lots of them came to school bare-footed, their clothes ragged and their stomachs empty. A report published in 1908 revealed that enormous numbers of children had bad teeth, bad eyesight, bad tonsils, bad hearing and various deformities due to rickets, ringworm, scabies and lice. So in the days before the WELFARE STATE schools were also responsible for trying to improve children's health by providing meals, baths and medical inspections. But for the rich, things were very different. They were expected to be the future leaders of the country, the owners of industry, the army officers and the rulers of the empire. No one thought for a moment that they should be educated in the ordinary schools and so their parents paid for them to attend public schools and grammar schools where they received a much better and more privileged education.

Schoolboys from Harrow public school.

PUBLIC SCHOOLS

Today the public schools still exist. About two and a half per cent of all fourteen-year-olds and nine per cent of all seventeen-year-olds at school in England and Wales attend public school. Not many, you may think, but with long waiting lists and expensive fees these pupils have something significant in common. Except for a few very intelligent children who win special scholarships they are usually the sons (and less often the daughters) of well-off and influential parents.

Teachers and politicians still argue about whether the public school system is fair. Some say that parents should be allowed to spend their money on expensive education for their children if they like. Others say that public schools give their pupils an unfair advantage over the majority of youngsters when it comes to passing exams and getting important jobs. Classes are smaller, pupils only mix with other wealthy children, and they stand a better chance of a highly paid and influential job later.

COMPREHENSIVE SCHOOLS

But most youngsters in Britain attend state secondary schools and here there have been a lot of changes — especially since the last war.

In recent years the main battle has been over comprehensive education — whether all children should go to the same school, regardless of their intelligence and upbringing, to receive the same opportunity to learn as everyone else, or whether children of different abilities should be put in different schools so that they can learn the things they are best suited for.

Now most state schools are comprehensive but in the 1960s the majority of pupils found themselves divided at eleven by an examination into either grammar schools or secondary modern schools. Your parents will know just how important it was to pass this exam at eleven and how discouraging it felt to fail. But only twenty to twenty-five percent were ever allowed to pass and most of the others didn't get as good an education as they deserved. The system was unfair and it was in an effort to remove this unfairness that comprehensives were introduced.

THE RAISING OF THE SCHOOL-LEAVING AGE

Another big change of recent years was the raising of the school-leaving age to sixteen in 1972. For many pupils who were anxious to get out to work it meant another year of 'prison'. Yet the decision was taken for a number of reasons.

The most important one was to do with social change. The modern world is changing rapidly. We know more today about science and technology and learning of all kinds more than ever before. New inventions and developments in industry all help to increase the speed of change. Who can tell what the world will be like in the year 2000? Many of the jobs we do now won't exist or will have been taken over by machines and computers. Our homes, holidays and leisure activities could be quite different. Look around the classroom in which you're sitting. You and your friends will be the workers and parents and organizers of that society. For this reason you need more and better education.

The other main reason you may find difficult to believe. The government in power in 1972 listened to the advice of many educational experts. A lot of them were teachers. They agreed that education was 'a good thing'. They thought that an educated person was likely to have a better life in the future than one who had learned little at school. And so it was decided that pupils should be made to stay on at school for an extra year.

A classroom in a comprehensive school.

RELATIONSHIPS BETWEEN TEACHERS AND PUPILS

The other big change has been in the relationship between pupils and teachers and in ways of learning. In general teachers today try to be friendlier to pupils than when your parents and grandparents were at school. They want pupils to learn because they're interested not because they're frightened of the teacher. They try to make their lessons more lively too, and encourage pupils to find out things for themselves. The old idea that there are a certain number of facts which children must know is rather out of date. Instead pupils need 'to learn how to learn'. They need to learn to ask questions and how to find out answers. They need to learn how to make choices.

48

HOW AND WHY?

Produce your own study in words and pictures of how and why schools have changed during the last hundred years. You will need to look at a number of different sources to build up a complete picture.

Here are some suggestions to help you.

1 How schools have changed . . .

Personal Accounts Interview your parents and grandparents about lessons, teachers and discipline when they were at school.	**Photographs** Pictures of school buildings, lessons, clothes, teachers and pupils can tell you a lot about the kind of schools there were.	**The Experts** Find out the facts from books and history teachers.

Finance
Ask a representative from the local authority:
How much is spent
on schools?
Where does the money
come from?
Is it enough?

Important Government Education Acts to find out about.

1870 Forster Educ. Act
1902 Balfour Educ. Act
1918 Fisher Educ. Act
1944 Butler Educ. Act
What changes did these acts bring about?

Different types of schools.
Elementary Schools
Primary Schools
Public Schools
Independent Schools
Grammar Schools
Technical Schools
Secondary Modern
   Schools
Comprehensive
   Schools

Why wouldn't it be enough *just* to ask your parents and grandparents about their memories of school?

2 Why schools have changed; ask the experts.

EDUCATIONAL EXPERTS
e.g. Headteacher

EMPLOYERS
e.g. Careers
adviser or local
personal manager

POLITICIANS
e.g. local MP,
Councillor or
representatives from
political parties

In finding out why schools have changed, why is it important to ask people concerned with jobs and politics as well as educational experts?

IS THERE A LAW AGAINST IT?

Answers to the questions on p. 45.

1 No. Most schools encourage parents to attend 'parents' evenings' but it's up to the school to make the first move.
2 No. A head can't insist on a particular uniform e.g. special tie, blazer, skirt etc. But a head can send home or refuse entry to a pupil he/she thinks isn't suitably dressed for school.
3 Yes. Teachers can put pupils in detention if they have a good reason to do so. But they should give the parents twenty four hours' notice. Most parents will accept the teachers decision but if they don't they can refuse permission.
4 Yes. But then the teacher becomes responsible for looking after the property. He/she can't keep it for ever — that would be theft.
5 Yes. So long as he/she doesn't cane enough to cause serious injury. But an increasing number of heads choose not to use the cane even though they have a legal right to do so.
6 They can complain but not forbid a head to use the cane on their child. The head has the right to keep discipline in whatever way he/she thinks is best.
7 No. They have no legal right to set homework but they can encourage pupils to do it if they think it's helpful. Some parents complain that their children don't get enough homework!
8 A good school might let pupils have some choice but in the last resort the teachers decide. A pupil is entered for GCE or CSE by the school which also pays the entry fee.
9 Yes. Especially if the pupils are wearing school uniform and can be identified by it.
10 The 1944 Education Act decided that Religious Knowledge should be compulsory in all schools. All other subjects are left to the individual schools to decide. Parents can write to the school and have their children excused from Religious Knowledge lessons if they have good reason.

WHAT HAPPENS TO THE GIRLS ?

Families are getting smaller. The average today is two or three children compared to six or seven a hundred years ago. At the beginning of the century a wife spent at least fifteen years of her life pregnant or nursing babies. Today it's more like four. Girls are marrying and having children. earlier. Before the war only ten per cent of girls married in their teens. Today the figure has risen to over thirty per cent. It's not surprising then, with less time spent in having babies and looking after them, that women are more involved in work outside the home. In deciding what that work will be, a lot depends on education and qualifications.

'It's time we stopped educating our women like men and producing imitation second-class males, because it's getting very difficult to get any one to do the domestic chores any more.'

Dr Edmund Leach, Keele University, 1969

Using the chart on pages 52-3 try answering these questions.

1 Suggest reasons why:
   a) Fewer girls than boys take CSE and GCE exams.
   b) Girls are more likely to leave school at sixteen than boys.
   c) Fewer girls than boys do apprenticeships and day-release courses.
2 What effects might girls'magazines and adverts have on discouraging girls from being 'too brainy' at school?
3 a) What kind of jobs are helped by studying science at school?
   b) Does it matter that more boys do science and more girls do commerce?
   c) Why should these examples always be given to suggest that girls don't get an equal chance in schools?
4 Do you agree or disagree with the view that boys should learn child-care and girls should learn car-maintenance in schools? Give full reasons for your answer.
5 Look at table 1.
   a) What percentage of pupils taking Home Economics examinations in 1972 were boys?
   b) What percentage of pupils taking Woodwork and Metalwork were girls?
   c) Look at the most recent edition of *Social Trends* to see whether examination entries in Home Economics and Metalwork and Woodwork have changed since 1972. Explain how.
7 What arguments would you use to either support or reject the parents' comment that it's more important to educate boys than girls?
8 Douglas, Ross and Simpson (see p. 53) suggest that girls are less ambitious than boys in the jobs they choose when they leave school. Do a survey of pupils' job ambitions in your class. Ask an equal number of boys and girls the questions.
   a) Is a well-paid job as important for girls as boys?

Yes	
Don't Know	
No	

   b) Is training and day release as important for girls as boys?

Yes	
No	
Don't Know	

   c) What job do you hope to get when you leave school?
   Write a report to explain the results of your survey commenting on whether or not it agrees with the findings of Douglas, Ross and Simpson (see page 53). Was there any difference between the views of boys and girls? Explain fully.
9 Try to find out whether boys and girls in your school get equal opportunities to learn. What methods of investigation will be best? Who can give you information? What questions will you need to have answered?
10 Suggest reasons why employers in 1972 were unwilling to give girls day release. What legislation introduced in December 1975 sought to change this? Write to a sample of local employers and to the local technical colleges to see whether things have changed since 1972.

At five boys and girls enter school.

At primary school they have the same lessons and do equally well, although some teachers expect different things from boys and girls.

Boys are more likely to do science; girls are more likely to do commerce.

At secondary school they often have different lessons.

Table 1
*Summer 1972 GCE, CSE &
Scottish Certificate of Education
Entries*

Subject	Girls	Boys
Home Economics	138000	2800
Woodwork & Metalwork	300	96000
Physics & Chemistry	88000	285000

(*Social Trends*, 1974)

Fewer girls enter for GCE and CSE than boys. But girls are more likely to pass their exams.

Table 2

CSE and GCE Summer Examinations: Entries and Results, England & Wales, Thousands & Percentages

| | 1962 | | 1972 | |
	Boys	Girls	Boys	Girls
Number of entries				
CSE Grade 1			742	608
GCE 'O' level	1 009	824	1 205	1 100
GCE 'A' level	184	86	279	188
Results (Percentage of entries)				
CSE Grade 1			15	17
GCE 'O' level pass	57	58	58	63
GCE 'A' level pass	66	70	68	71

(Source: *Statistics of Education*)

Girls are more likely to leave school at sixteen than boys.

'Between eleven and sixteen boys become increasingly aware that what they learn at school will influence their future careers and the sort of employment open to them on leaving school. In contrast the girls see themselves entering work which requires little training and which will last only a few years before marriage.'

(*All Our Future*, by Douglas, Ross and Simpson)

On leaving school at sixteen roughly forty-two percent of boys and only seven percent of girls do apprenticeships.

'That employers are unwilling to give girls day-release is well known. Only ten percent of young women in work compared to forty percent of young men receive day release.'

(*Discrimination Against Women* Labour Party Green Paper 1972)

'I really wanted to be a mechanic, but there were no apprenticeships for women.'

BRIAN'S SCHOOL REPORT

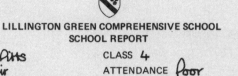

LILLINGTON GREEN COMPREHENSIVE SCHOOL
SCHOOL REPORT

NAME *Brian Pitts*   CLASS **4**

CONDUCT *Fair*   ATTENDANCE *Poor*

Form Tutor's Remarks

Brian seems only interested in school when games are being played. He is unwilling to do written work and is frequently absent without good reason. He has already been withdrawn from Maths C.S.E. and unless he improves in other subjects his results next year will be very poor.

SUBJECT	EXAM MARK	TERM GRADE	TEACHERS COMMENTS
English	49	C	*Brian never does any homework, but always has something good to say in class discussion. There is a lot of work missing from his C.S.E. folder*
Maths	31	D	*Brian has missed a lot of work this term because of poor attendance it will not be entered for CSE.*
Social Studies	45	C	*Brian finds it hard to concentrate and is easily distracted by his friends.*
Art and Design	78	B	*Brian has produced some excellent pottery this term but seems embarrassed to admit it.*
Games		A	*As captain of the first XI, Brian has had a very good season. He has scored consistently and encouraged his team to play well.*

Brian's Average Weekly Income

Pocket money from Dad	1.00
Pocket money from Mum	75
Saturday job	2.00
TOTAL	£3.75

Brian's Average Weekly Expenditure

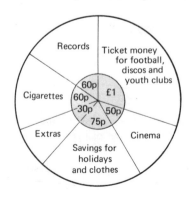

Records

Ticket money for football, discos and youth clubs

Cigarettes

60p

60p

£1

30p

50p

75p

Cinema

Extras

Savings for holidays and clothes

Dear Mr Warwick,

I am sorry Brian's report was so bad. We did not know he was missing school and his father has punished him. We will try to make sure that he does his home work before he goes out at night, though some of his friends don't help. He never seems to tell us what he's up to these days, but his father would keep him in for good if he thought it was any more police trouble. Thank you for your advice.

Yours truly,
Ellen Pitts (Mrs)

(Probation Officer – M.D.Richards)

NAME   Brian Pitts

OFFENCE   Fighting and carrying a dangerous weapon at a football match

PENALTY   Two years' probation

December 19th

Brian came to see me today and told me about his bad school report. He had been kept in for a week by his father and is now forced to do homework every night. He seems a bright lad—not incapable of working but just bored with school. His poor attendance worried me. 'Where do you go to?' I asked. He claims to a friend's house to listen to records and practise the guitar. They're starting a pop group. I asked him if he still supports United. 'Of course', he said, 'but no fighting now – that's for kids. I've got to keep fit for the school team.'

Lillington Green School made sure of the Under 16s Football Trophy today when skipper Brian Pitts pushed home two quick goals in their seventh round match against Bilston Boys. Lillington looked on top from the start but it needed the goal-scoring drive of Pitts to keep out Bilston who never looked like giving up. Their two-nil win has put Lillington well ahead, needing only one more point from their next two games to take the cup.

WHAT DO YOU EXPECT FROM SCHOOL ?

Maybe you know some boys and girls like Brian — not unintelligent but a bit fed up with school, more interested in pop music and football. He wants to leave school as soon as he can, but his parents are keen for him to get a good job and that means taking examinations. Mr Warwick, his class teacher, also thinks that passing exams is important — more important than being good at football or playing in a pop group. 'Why can't I do both?' Brian wants to know. 'Get CSEs in games and study pop in school music lessons. They do in some schools.'

Part of the problem lies in the fact that people disagree on what they expect from a school. Is it to fill pupils' heads full of knowledge? Is it to help them get a good job? Has it anything to do with learning to be a good citizen? Should it help them to stand up for what they believe in or speak out against what is bad in society?

1 Discuss together all the information you have on Brian and then answer these questions giving reasons for your views.

   a) Do you think his school report is bad?

   b) Is he a boring person with few interests and no talents?

   c) Why do you think that he often gets fed up with school?

   d) What do his weekly 'income' and 'expenditure' tell you about him?

   e) What advice would you give to Brian, his parents, teacher and probation officer?

2 Look at the list of things schools do. Add any others you think have been left out.

   a) Put them in the order you think is best with the most important first.

   b) Try out the list on a sample of teachers and a sample of parents and then compare their opinions with those of you and your friends.

THINGS SCHOOLS TRY TO DO	Order of Importance
Help you do as well as possible in examinations like GCE or CSE.	
Teach you things which will be of direct use to you in your job.	
Teach you things which will help you to get as good a job or career as possible.	
Teach you about different sorts of jobs and careers so that you can decide what you want to do.	
Help you to know what it will be like when you start work, for example, about hours and conditions.	
Teach you things that will be useful in running a home, for example, about bringing up children home repairs, decorating.	
Teach you how to manage your money when you are earning, and about things like rates and income tax.	
Give sex education.	
Help you to learn how to get on with other people, for example, those you work with, your future wife or husband.	
Teach you to speak well and easily.	
Teach you to be able to put things in writing easily.	
Help you to become independent and able to stand on your own feet.	
Help you develop your personality and character.	
Teach you about what is right and wrong.	
Help you to make the most of yourself, for example, with your appearance.	
Help you to know about what is going on in the world nowadays.	
Give you interests and hobbies that you can do in your spare time.	
Run clubs that you can go to out of school hours.	
Take you away on holidays.	
Arrange courses in which you live away from home for a while.	
Take you on outings to places like art galleries, the theatre, museums or castles.	
Teach you drama in school, that is, acting or reading plays.	
Teach you to study poetry in school and read or learn poems.	

ROLE CONFLICT FOR YASMEEN

One in four babies born in Huddersfield these days belongs to parents who've come from other countries. It's likely that their roles * will be even more confusing to learn than those of English children. Take Yasmeen, for example. She is a Moslem — a believer in a religion called Islam which dates back 1300 years and which exercises a strict and traditional discipline on its followers, even when they live in a largely non-Moslem country like Britain.

Pakistani families in Huddersfield obviously want to keep their religion and all its traditions and beliefs alive. Houses and converted chapels often serve as *mosques.* Young boys are taken there by their fathers and learn to read the *Koran* in Arabic. They learn the religious meaning of *ritual purification* and how to pray facing *Mecca,* the holy city of *Mohammed,* in a way which dates back for generations.

At home the power in the family is with the elderly. When Yasmeen and her brothers sit down to eat they speak only when they're spoken to and everyone abides by the advice and decisions of her grandfather.

Moslem law allows polygamy, or the right of a man to have up to four wives. Not all Moslem men take advantage of this, especially in Britain, but Yasmeen's father has two. According to Moslem law, each wife is entitled to equal love and equal space in the home, something which is quite difficult in an already overcrowded terraced house in Huddersfield. But that's not the only problem. Since British law only recognizes the rights of one wife, Yasmeen's father cannot claim tax allowances and benefits for his second wife, and her two children are considered by British law to be illegitimate.

The lives and responsibilities of men and women in the Moslem world are very different. Women aren't expected to work outside the home — cooking, rearing children and looking after their husbands are their traditional duties. Few Moslem women in Huddersfield contradict these rules. Many of them don't speak English for they have no need to learn.

The children must go to school, however, and this is often where some of the problems begin. The world of school to Yasmeen is very different from the world of home. She comes into contact every day with British teenagers and a society which is much more permissive and unrestricted than her own. She loves the friendliness of her classmates and enjoys all her lessons, especially science and games. But when her friends go out to the pictures or the youth club disco, she's not allowed to join in.

Boyfriends are out of the question as far as her parents are concerned and short skirts, dancing and the latest fashions are thought to be almost 'sinful' in the deeply religious Moslem community. Traditional Moslems are shocked by what they see as permissiveness and violence in British society — especially among the young. And while their sons are thought to be strong enough to resist these temptations and to go out unaccompanied, their daughters are not.

For Yasmeen her time at school is a short period of freedom. When she leaves next year she won't be allowed to get a job. She must stay and help the women at home until she is ready to be married.

* To remind yourselves about roles and role conflict look back to page 9.

USING BOOKS FROM THE LIBRARY *

1 Make detailed notes on Islam, Mohammed, Mecca, the Koran, mosques, purification and polygamy.

2 What is the problem with polygamy in British law?

3 In which countries of the world is Islam the main religion?

4 Why, in Moslem society, is power with the elderly rather than the young, and with men rather than women? Explain as fully as you can how this compares with Britain.

5 Religious education and some form of daily worship is compulsory in British schools. In schools where there are pupils from other countries, how much effort should be made to study and practise their religions? Is it important that British students should learn about the history, geography, stories and traditions of countries like India, Bangladesh and Pakistan? Give full reasons for your answers.

6 The meals a Moslem teenager takes at home are very different from the dinners they may have at school. Pakistani food is much spicier and school dinners must taste very dull in comparison. There are also religious restrictions on what Moslems are allowed to eat and not allowed to eat.
   a) What are these restrictions and what is the reason for them?
   b) Make a collection of pictures and recipes of Indian and Pakistani food. Ask your teacher if you can try some of them out in cookery lessons.

7 Put yourselves in the shoes of a Pakistani Moslem family living in Huddersfield. Why might they think of British society as 'permissive' and 'violent'? Is there any evidence to support their beliefs about Britain?

8 Some things are good about being a teenager in Britain, some bad. Which things would you most like to share with Yasmeen? Which things is she better off without?

9 Explain as fully as you can why Yasmeen's different roles of daughter, pupil and schoolfriend may often be in conflict with each other. Who has most influence on her? To whom should she listen? What would you do in her place?

10 'No one wants Moslems in Britain to forget their religion and be exactly like us. But to survive here they'll have to give way on a few things.' How far do you agree with this view? What pressures may force the Moslem community in Britain to give more freedom to their women and their young people?

Moslems in Britain meeting to pray in a converted hall in Woking.

* You can also get useful information by writing to the Community Relations Commission (see p.160).

WHAT MAKES A GOOD TEACHER?

I must not bore children
I must not bore children
I must not b

1 Look at the chart below. There are twenty-five statements made by
   pupils and teachers about what they think makes a good teacher.
   Consider each one carefully.
2 Put a tick in the column marked ✓ against the six qualities which you
   think are most important.
3 Now decide which of your six choices you think is most important
   and which is least important. In the column headed 'order of
   importance', give the most important six marks, the next five, the
   next four and so on down to one mark.
4 Count up the scores for the class as a whole and find out which six
   qualities get the highest number of marks.
5 Now try the choices out on a sample of parents and teachers. (If
   thirty pupils took part, you should also ask thirty teachers and thirty
   parents.) In the same way as before find out which six qualities get
   the highest number of marks from parents and teachers.
6 Write a report to compare and contrast what pupils, teachers and
   parents think about what makes a good teacher.

CHARACTERISTICS	✓	ORDER OF IMPORTANCE
1 A good teacher is patient, understanding, kind and sympathetic.		
2 A good teacher is young in heart.		
3 A good teacher uses the cane or strap when necessary.		
4 A good teacher knows where to find the things he/she wants.		
5 A good teacher encourages you to work hard at school.		
6 A good teacher knows a great deal about the subject he/she is teaching.		
7 A good teacher is cheerful and good-tempered.		
8 A good teacher takes an interest in you as an individual.		
9 A good teacher makes certain that the classroom is tidy and attractive.		
10 A good teacher is strict and doesn't allow 'playing about'.		
11 A good teacher has no favourites.		
12 A good teacher explains the work you have to do and helps you with it.		
13 A good teacher is able to organize all kinds of activities in the classroom.		
14 A good teacher lets you have some of your own way.		
15 A good teacher has work ready for you as soon as you get into the classroom.		
16 A good teacher looks nice and dresses well.		
17 A good teacher gives interesting lessons.		
18 A good teacher makes sure you have the pens, paper and books you need.		
19 A good teacher never uses corporal punishment.		
20 A good teacher gives you time in the lesson to finish your work.		
21 A good teacher has a sense of humour.		
22 A good teacher is well-mannered and polite.		
23 A good teacher is interested in your opinion.		
24 A good teacher is friendly with pupils in and out of school.		
25 A good teacher praises you for behaving well and working hard.		

(Adapted from *Society and the Teachers' Role* by Musgrove and Taylor.)

1

This headteacher is saying one thing and thinking another. Can you explain why? What are the reasons for and against school uniform?

Imagine that a special parent-teachers' meeting has been called to discuss school uniform. Prepare a speech on whether to keep school uniform or to abolish it from the point of view of:

a) The headteacher.
b) Two teachers with different opinions.
c) One of the school governors.
d) Two parents with different opinions.
e) One or two of the pupils.

2

WHAT'S YOUR OPINION?

Here are the views of four teenagers on things that happen in schools. Think about each opinion carefully and then say whether or not you agree, giving full reasons for your answer.

'I hope that all the schools of tomorrow will have much more freedom and variety than those of today. By freedom I mean much more time to work individually on subjects that pupils find interesting; and by variety I mean more flexibility in the weekly prog- ramme of lessons.'
Gillian, 14

'Homework should not be given. Many of us would rather spend another hour at school than two hours at home doing 'an hour's homework', where we are constantly being distracted by television and such things.'
Irene, 15.

'I would like assemblies to become voluntary. This is not because then I could get out of going to assembly, but because religion is one thing that should not be forced on anybody.'
Carol, 14.

'Prefects are rarely chosen wisely. They seem to let their new powers go to their heads. My ideal would be for the pupils to elect their own prefects. Or better still have none at all. If one select group of pupils is given all the responsibilities, there's no chance for anyone else.
Nicholas 15

1 How many days a year must you spend receiving education?
2 Is it legal for parents to educate their children at home?
3 Which Education Act made Religious Knowledge the only compulsory subject in school?
4 When was the school-leaving age raised to fourteen?
5 When was the school-leaving age raised to sixteen?
6 What was the 'half-time system' and when did it operate?
7 What percentage of fourteen-year-olds and seventeen-year-olds go to public school in England and Wales?
8 What was the difference between grammar schools and secondary modern schools?
9 What is meant by the term 'polygamy'?
10 What is meant by the term 'role conflict'?

1 SITE IMPROVEMENTS

Pupils in some parts of Liverpool go to schools built in the last century. These are very old and very ugly. So the pupils decided, with the help of their teachers, to improve them by painting big colourful paintings on the inside of the playground walls. In schools which have no playing fields or gardens it would also be possible to plant flowers and creepers in tubs and barrels.

Some old churches and community centres could also do with brightening up.

Find out if there are any old schools, churches or other buildings in the area which would like a face-lift and see if you can help.

2 TRAVELLING EXHIBITIONS

It's a good idea to let local people see what you have discovered in your various surveys and investigations. One way of letting them know is to have an open day and exhibition. But often only parents are invited to these and sometimes they can't come for various reasons.

Much better to take your exhibition to the people. See whether one of the local shops will let you use their window. All the better if it's a shop which lots of people use or pass by during the day. Perhaps a local factory or a pub will let you put up a display too.

3 COMMUNITY CONCERNS

In a school in Hull the pupils and their teacher wanted to discuss some of the problems in their area with local residents and the council. So they arranged a series of discussion meetings on 'Community Concerns'. They included education, housing, work, the environment and many others. Posters were put in local shops and pupils delivered leaflets round the doors.

Each Monday evening a big group of local people and pupils from the school met to discuss important issues with local councillors. Never before had local people had this kind of opportunity and the meetings were a great success.

Help to arrange a series of similar events in your area.

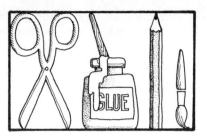

1

You've seen cartoons used a lot in this chapter — partly to amuse you, partly to illustrate important points. Produce some cartoons of your own on 'Schools Today'.

2

What do you think it's like to be a student teacher? Find out what their training involves. What qualifications do they need to become real teachers?

3

Ask your teacher to help you make contact with a school in another part of Britain or in another country. Make a comparison in words, drawings, photographs and tapes between that school and yours.

4

Make a study of public schools in Britain. Find out about their history, traditions, privileges and punishments. What are the advantages and disadvantages of going to public school?

5

Some pupils would rather play truant than go to school. There are lots of reasons why they dislike school — boredom, fear, laziness, family problems. You can probably suggest others. But who's to blame? The parents? The pupils? The schools? or a mixture of all three? Imagine you have to make a TV programme about truancy for 'World in Action' or 'Man Alive'. You can produce it on tape with charts, photographs, drawings and slides for illustration if filming is impossible. Try to present all points of view fairly by interviewing pupils, parents, teachers and social-workers. What do the truants do and where do they go when they're not at school? Why is truancy thought to be a problem? What — if anything — could be done to make schools more appealing to the truants?

6

In South Africa, all white children between seven and sixteen must go to school.

Seventy percent of all black children leave school at eight.

Five percent of black children stay at school until twelve.

The South African government spends 258 Rand per year on each white child's education and 19 Rand per year on each black child's education in government schools.

Find out about the different ways in which whites and blacks are treated in South Africa.
Where do they live and work?
What legal rights do they have?
Has the government's spending or attitude to educational opportunities changed in recent years?

The population of South Africa is 25 000 000.
Seventy percent are black Africans
Eighteen percent are white.
Nine percent are half-castes.
Three percent are Asian.

5 TEENAGE TRENDS

Being a teenager is the period in your life when you stop being a child and start taking on the rights and responsibilities of an adult.

Of course things don't happen overnight. The law takes longer to recognize that you're an adult in some things than others. And in some ways it can seem inconsistent.

For instance, you can get married (with your parents' consent) at sixteen, but you can't buy drinks in a pub until you're eighteen. A boy of fourteen can be convicted of rape and is thought adult enough to be responsible for any other crimes he might commit. But until sixteen he is still regarded as a schoolboy and he isn't thought old enough to vote until eighteen. Girls reach 'the age of consent' for sexual intercourse at sixteen, though the 'age of majority', when the law says they can leave home, apply for a passport, take on hire purchase, sit on a jury and pay adult contributions to National Insurance schemes, is not until eighteen.

All of these mean that the law's recognition of you being an adult is quite a bit later than when biologically you stop being a child and become capable of reproduction. Can you think of any reasons for this?

Sometimes the 'waiting around' to be seen as an adult can be irritating. Often parents and teachers keep telling you to 'act your age' and 'behave like an adult'. Yet in terms of their rules and regulations, they may still be treating you like children. On the other hand, with a lifetime of marriage, work and responsibilities to look forward to, it can be fun to do childish things now and again and to enjoy your years as a teenager.

SO WHAT ARE YOU INTERESTED IN ?

The mass media — newspapers, television, and the cinema — are all important in today's world. But so far as teenagers are concerned, the most influential media are to do with pop and fashion. Teenagers don't read many newspapers, and they watch less TV than any other age group. According to research, though, 'Top of the Pops' is their favourite programme. Radio 1 is also popular, and weekly magazines about romance, pop and fashion sell in their thousands. *Jackie,* the best-selling magazine for girls, claims over a million readers each week.

So from this information it's fair to suggest that pop, romance, and fashion play a very big part in teenagers' lives. Though of course not the only part. Two sociologists, Murdock and Phelps, have made a study of *Mass Media and the Secondary Schools* and they suggest that pop media and the schools are in competition for young people's attention. This letter to *Jackie* illustrates this point.

Counting the Minutes

I'd like to thank all you folks at *Jackie* for giving me, a poor hardworking schoolgirl, 6 240 minutes of reading a year, out of 43 360 minutes of schoolwork!

Louise Kerr,
York

Jackie 26.4.75

THE RESEARCH FINDINGS

For some young people school is all important. They enjoy it during the day, attend clubs there in the evening or do homework regularly. But many teenagers aren't satisfied with what school has to offer and look for other activities and interests to get involved in.

Murdock and Phelps suggest that there are two alternative sets of activities open to young people:
1 neighbourhood friends, clubs and coffee bars and supporting the local football team.
2 all the trappings of the media pop industry — records, fashion and magazines.

They claim that youngsters who get most involved in pop are either middle class teenagers who aren't very interested or very successful at school, or working class girls who don't belong to neighbourhood gangs.

When it comes to school, Murdock and Phelps suggest that there's a huge gap between pupils' and teachers' attitudes to the media. For example, teachers are more likely to read serious newspapers and less likely to watch TV than either their pupils or the general public.

Teachers are also less likely either to listen to pop music or to enjoy it than pupils. When interviewed, some young teachers said they did listen to pop music, but most of them felt it was trivial and a waste of time. Some even felt that it had a harmful effect on their pupils.

The fact that most teachers did not share their pupils' interest in pop, and knew very little about the pop their pupils were interested in, led Murdock and Phelps to suggest that this ignorance could aggravate and widen the gap between pupils and teachers.

YOUR OWN RESEARCH

Murdock and Phelps raise some interesting points with which you might or might not agree. They also leave certain questions unanswered. Carry out a piece of research of your own among teenagers and teachers to test their findings.
Here are some suggestions to help you:
1 a) Make a questionnaire to find out how young people spend their leisure time and to see whether pop, fashion and romance are the most important things in their lives.
   b) What other activities not mentioned by Murdock and Phelps take up a lot of time?
   c) Do social class, age or sex make any difference to the ways in which teenagers spend their leisure time?

2 a) Murdock and Phelps talk about middle class teenagers. Look back to p.65.

   b) Why are middle-class teenagers who aren't so successful at school and working-class girls likely to be most involved in pop?

   c) How could you test whether this view is correct?

3 a) Make a questionnaire for teachers to test their knowledge of pop music, how often they listen to pop and their attitudes to it.

   b) Does the age group of the teacher make any difference here?

4 a) Does your school try to share in or to avoid the world of pop and teenage fashions?

   b) Give it a mark from 1 to 10 on this Pop Appeal Chart.

   c) Write a report to explain fully why you have given the school either a high or low mark.

POP APPEAL	Rating 1 – 10
Teachers who are knowledgeable about and interested in the pop media.	
Lessons in which pupils and teachers discuss the world of pop.	
Attitudes to school uniform which take account of the latest fashions.	
School-run discos and record sessions.	
The opportunity to learn to play pop instruments.	
Useful tips on fashion sense for boys and girls.	
Help and advice with personal relationships.	

THE POP BUSINESS

In a competition organized by a radio station in America, a fourteen-year-old girl said, 'I think he is one of the greatest things that ever happened to teenage America.' Can you guess whom she was referring to?

In fact the competition was almost thirty years ago and she meant Frank Sinatra.

A lot has happened to popular music since then. Those people who say it all sounds the same are wrong. And those who say it's trivial and unimportant forget just how big a part it plays in the lives of most young people in Britain today.

Because it's so important, you should try to find out as much about it as you can, both the good things and the bad.

WHO WANTS TO BE A MILLIONAIRE?

> GOOD-LOOKING male musicians and singer aged between 16 and 20 to form exciting new pop group. Send full details and photo to management record company. Box 304

Answering an advert like this is how some pop stars begin their careers. But for every one who goes on to make a hit record, thousands more never get any further than the advertising columns of the musical press.

Becoming a pop star may be the dream of many a teenager but it's not always as exciting as this advert promises. The pop world can also be tough, phoney and immoral. But for those who don't mind all that there is obviously plenty of money to be made.

Here's the view of Ronald Cave and Raymond O'Malley:

'It would be pleasant to think of pop groups as groups of young people fond of music and entertainment, playing for the love of it and winning fame and wealth almost without meaning to. The first part of the description is doubtless true, in the case of some pop groups, but the rest is very wide of the mark.

'The rise of a pop group is a matter of ruthless, competitive money-spending in the hope of money-making. Behind the smiling (or sometimes scowling) faces of the singers, guitarists and drummers, there are other unseen faces — those of managers, agents, publicity experts, financial backers, record-company directors, highly paid TV men and contact agents. music publishers, agents and, of course, the ever-present disc jockeys. An astonishing amount of money is spent — tens of thousands of pounds — in ways that are never mentioned to the pop-loving public.'

(*Living with the Mass Media*)

Stardust
In his book, *Stardust*, Ray Conolly takes a look at the rise of a young pop star.

'And so the whole band-waggon of money and work rolled through the year. Gigs were played, film parts were offered and turned down, television shows were done, a tour of Europe was a sell-out in Germany, Holland and Denmark. . . . And all the time there was recording to be done, cars to be bought, clothes to be fitted for, journalists to be seen and endless legal hassles to be sorted out with lawyers. . . .

'Getting a tour on the road was like organizing a small army — hiring lighting men, sound technicians, drivers, dope-pedlars, and the best people in stage make-up, security and love-making. No matter what the time or the place the girls had to be available. . . .

'Belle Vue, like every other date he had played, was the same hectic nightmare of chaos, screaming, hysterical girls, loud, out-of-tune music and then the inevitable hiding on the floor of the Daimler as it tried to force a way through the police barriers and the ecstatic crowds. . . .

'Sometimes a misguided or over-avid fan would throw a firework towards the stage in excitement and mindful of the risks of assassination, police would tear into the crowds to drag out the bruised and screaming protester. By the sides of the stage rows of cripples would queue in their wheelchairs, waiting to be touched by the pretty messiah. Civic heads would stand proudly with sprightly daughters to reap a perk of their profession and get to meet the visiting star. And Red Indians, cowboys or Eskimos (depending upon the location) would further debase their histories by being photographed for the local papers presenting head-dresses, holsters and guns or fur skins. No promotional stone was left unturned in the drive for vast profitability and nothing was too phoney for him to agree to. Within four months he became all things to all men; as cute as a Monkee; as mean as a Jagger, as intelligent as a Dylan and as plastic as a Beatle.'

(Adapted from *Stardust*, by Ray Connolly)

Choose a pop group and make a detailed study of its career. Try to find out about those behind the scenes who have helped to make it successful. (You can choose a solo performer if you'd rather.)

1 How did the group get started in the pop business?
2 How many hits have they had and how long have they been popular?

3 Who is their manager? What other stars is he/she responsible for? What does his/her job involve?

4 a) Which record company issues their records?

b) See if you can find out any details of their contract with the record company and what percentage of their earnings is taken by the record company and their manager.

c) What goes on in the record company's promotion department?

d) What is the job of the A & R Man (Arrangement and Repertoire)?

e) What kind of activities are handled by the press office?

5 a) Make a collection of magazine features and news stories about the group you've chosen.

b) What kind of 'image' is being presented in these cuttings?

6 Describe any publicity stunts or promotion drives that have been organized to draw attention to the group.

7 In what ways have television, concerts, radio and disc jockeys contributed to making the group popular?

8 What aspect of the group's behaviour do you think is most likable? Are there any aspects which you think are unpleasant? What evidence do you have for these views? Give details and explain the reasons for your approval or disapproval.

POP WORDS
Future Legend

'And . . . In the death — as the last few corpses lay rotting on the slimy thoroughfare — the shutters lifted in inches in Temperance Building — high on Poachers Hill and red mutant eyes gazed down on Hunger City — no more big wheels — fleas the size of rats sucked on rats the size of cats and ten thousand peoploids split into small tribes coveting the highest of the sterile skyscrapers — like packs of dogs assaulting the glass fronts of Love Me Avenue — ripping and re-wrapping mink and shiny silver fox — now leg warmers — family badge of sapphire and creaked emerald — any day now — the year of the Diamond Dogs.'

'This ain't Rock n' Roll —
this is Genocide.'   David Bowie 1974

This rather disturbing verse begins side one of David Bowie's Diamond Dogs LP.

1 Read it together carefully. What is it about?
2 What kind of picture does it bring to your mind?
3 Does it remind you of anything?
4 What kind of shapes and colours does it suggest?

5 How do you imagine the buildings and the faces of the people would look?
6 Make a painting or a model to illustrate Bowie's Future Legend.

Because of the beat and rhythm of pop music, some people forget about the words. But they can be quite important. Here are two contrasting opinions about the value of pop song words:

'The words themselves are almost the most dismal part of pop music. The title of the song is very important, and will reappear at different times in the song with something of the regularity of an advertising slogan. This means that there will be little danger of any teenager forgetting the name of a song when ordering it from a record shop. The moods of most songs vary each year according to the style of music, but love is the centre around which the theme and action revolve. Tears are commonly mentioned in such songs; and in this way many teenagers can express feelings that they may feel inhibited about showing or discussing. It is no wonder that people who find it difficult to express themselves in words may turn to records to do it for them.'
(Nicholas Tucker, *Understanding the Mass Media*)

'A fifteen-year-old boy takes a hit song, "My Name is Jack", and creates his own poem, achieving a deep empathy for one of the social rejects of Spitalfields or Whitechapel . . . . Another takes a sentimental song like "Grandad", and recreates it as a sympathetic insight into the experience of old age . . . . Commercial pop music had turned to poetry; promoting sympathy and mutual understanding.'
(Chris Searle, *This New Season*)

1 Explain carefully what each writer is suggesting and say how far you agree or disagree with him.

2 Choose two or three of your favourite hit songs of the moment. Write down the words of the songs and say whether you think they're good or not. Why?

3 Have the lyrics been chosen to communicate any particular message to the audience or just to fit in with the tune? Explain how.

4 Do the words have any special meaning for you? Why?

5 Which of the lyrics do you think is a) most commercial b) most sincere and c) most imaginative? Why?

6 Choose one of your favourite pop tunes of the moment and try writing your own words to fit it. See how different and how much better than the original you can make your version of the lyric.

GROUPS AND GANGS

A well-known characteristic of teenagers during the last twenty years or so has been their association with different GANGS and YOUTH MOVEMENTS. There were gangs before the war, of course, but never on such a large scale as today. Unlike the pre-war gangs which developed out of the desperation of poverty and unemployment, the youth movements of recent years have involved more people and spread largely because of affluence.

Teenagers today have more money than ever before to spend on the latest fashions and crazes, and in providing clothes, music and leisure activities for them, businessmen and commercial interests have been able to make a lot of money.

Television, radio, newspapers and magazines have also played their part. By giving lots of publicity to both the good and bad aspects of gang behaviour they've encouraged them to spread. But being part of a gang obviously appeals to teenagers too. Having a group to identify with and spend time with is important, especially if school and the older generation of parents seem out of touch and not interested in the things you enjoy.

You probably know the names of some of the main movements since the war. The best known have been Teddy Boys, Mods and Rockers, Hell's Angels, Hippies and Jesus Freaks, Skinheads, Suedeheads, Boot Boys and Punk Rockers.

MODS AND ROCKERS

The mid-60s was the age of the Mods and Rockers, two groups who attracted thousands of teenage members and loyal supporters. A good deal of rivalry grew up between them in terms of dress, attitudes, musical tastes and types of behaviour. And sometimes this rivalry led to violence.

The rivalry certainly pleased commercial interests. Carnaby Street encouraged and supplied Mod fashions and became world-famous for its trendy clothes and 'swinging' image. Five top-selling magazines started up to supply pop and fashion information purely for Mods. The Rockers too had their own music, motorbikes and style of clothing.

But whether the rivalry would have led to violence without the encouragement of newsapapers and television is hard to say.

The scene for the first of the major battles was Clacton, a small holiday resort on the east coast of England. There wasn't much to do there if the weather was bad, and Easter 1964, as sociologist Stanley Cohen describes, was worse than usual.

'It was cold and wet and in fact Easter Sunday was the coldest for eighty years. The shop-keepers and stall owners were irritated by lack of business. The young people who gathered there for the holiday weekend were bored. There were rumours that

some café-owners and barmen were refusing to serve some of them. A few groups started shuffling on the pavement and throwing stones at each other. The Mods and Rockers, identifiable by their different clothes, started separating out. Those on bikes and scooters roared up and down, windows were broken, some beach huts were wrecked and one boy fired a starting pistol in the air. The large numbers of people, the disappointment over the weather, the boredom, the general irritation and some of the actions of the unprepared and undermanned police force all contributed to the unpleasantness'.

On the Monday following the incidents at Clacton, every national newspaper except *The Times* carried a leading report on the weekend's events. The headlines speak for themselves; *DAY OF TERROR BY SCOOTER GROUPS (Daily Telegraph), YOUNGSTERS BEAT UP TOWN — 97 LEATHER JACKET ARRESTS (Daily Express), WILD ONES INVADE SEA-SIDE — 97 ARRESTS (Daily Mirror)*. These were followed by articles claiming to include interviews with Mods and Rockers. In all of them it was very difficult to sort out what was fact and what was opinion. Newsmen described the 'mobs' as 'exhilarated', 'drunk with notoriety', 'hell bent for destruction', etc. Sensational headlines grossly over-exaggerated the seriousness of the events, the numbers involved and the amount of damage done. The regular use of phrases like 'riot', 'orgy of destruction', 'battle', 'attack', 'siege', 'beat up the town' and 'screaming mob' all

helped to paint the picture of innocent holiday makers fleeing in terror from rioting teenagers.

This kind of newspaper reporting made things worse for the future. It meant that all those involved — young people, the police and the general public — all expected there to be trouble whenever Mods and Rockers came face to face. Rumours were believed, insults imagined and incidents inevitably flared up.

HIPPIES

A different group of slightly older teenagers copied a movement that was very important in America in the mid-sixties, the Hippies . Hippies, or Flower

Children as they sometimes called themselves, were opposed to what they saw as the 'rat race' in America: the pressure to get on, to spend money, to amass lots of possessions, to be respectable. They also objected to the violence they saw around them, violence against Negroes and by American soldiers in Vietnam. Their message was to 'make love not war'.

But while the Hippies preached peace, the search for new experiences through meditation and drugs, and the 'dropping-out' of the rat race, commercial America made a fortune out of selling them the clothes, beads, music, and drugs which characterized the movement.

JESUS FREAKS

In 1966 John Lennon had said the Beatles were more popular than Jesus but by 1971 there was a surprising swing back to Christianity among young people and ex-Beatle George Harrison had a hit with 'My Sweet Lord'.

The movement started in America about 1967. Teenagers who had once taken drugs now talked of 'getting high on Jesus' and 'turning on to the Lord'. All the techniques of an expertly-organized advertising campaign were used to spread the word 1970s style. Jesus-stickers and badges proclaimed, 'Smile, Jesus loves you'. There was a Jesus sign — the clenched fist with one finger pointing heavenwards, a Jesus cheer — give me a J, give me a E, give me an S, etc. There was even a Jesus wrist-watch.

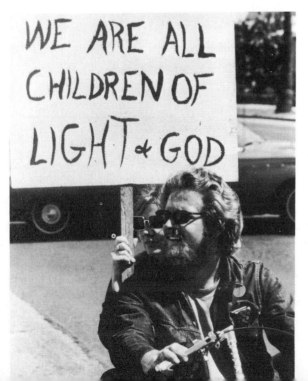

In 1971 the Jesus movement came to Britain. Arthur Blessit, a Baptist Minister from Los Angeles, who used a mixture of pop, drugs and religious terms, conducted services in an atmosphere more like a club than a church. In America he had been famous for his 'toilet services' in which he invited the congregation of one-time Hippies to flush their pills and assorted drugs down the lavatory.

Rock operas like 'Godspell' and 'Jesus Christ Superstar' all helped to make sure that the old message of Christianity was brought bang up to date and publicity increased when Cliff Richard joined the Festival of Light and Pat Boone started baptising people in his swimming pool. Even the older generation got in on the act.

1 Make a detailed study of your own of any of the youth groups mentioned above.
   a) How did they come together in the first place?
   b) What was special about their dress, attitudes and activities?
   c) How did the mass media and commercial interests react to them?
   d) How did the older generation react to them?
2 The most popular groups of recent years, Skinheads and Boot Boys, seem to have had a number of things in common:
   a) They tended to appeal to younger teenagers (thirteen to sixteen) rather than older ones.
   b) Members tended to be boys rather than girls.
   c) Fighting seemed to be one of their main activities.
   d) They seemed to despise foreigners, especially Indians and Pakistanis. Suggest reasons for this from your own experience.
3 Which teenage youth movements are most common today? Describe the clothes, attitudes and activities, as fully as you can.
4 All of the youth movements we've talked about so far were more or less started by young people, even if they were later encouraged and spread by commercial interests and the mass media. But some youth movements have been deliberately started by the older generation. The Boy Scouts, the Hitler Youth and the Red Guards in China are three such examples.
   Find out as much as you can about any of these groups and try to explain exactly why the older generation founded and encouraged them.

HOW OFTEN ARE YOU TAKEN IN BY THE AD-MAN?

Before answering the question, fill in this questionnaire as HONESTLY as you can. In each case, tick the answer which is CLOSEST to your own feelings and opinions. Add up your score at the end.

FACING UP TO YOURSELF			
1. Do you ever feel self-conscious about being too tall, too small, too fat or too thin?	a) often b) sometimes c) never		
2. When you meet someone of the opposite sex for the first time, what's the first thing you notice about them?	a) Whether they're good looking or not b) Whether they're intelligent or not c) Whether they have a nice personality or not		
3. If your boyfriend/girlfriend saw you not looking your best, would you	a) feel very self-conscious and try to hide? b) feel a bit embarrassed and make apologies for your appearance? c) not feel the slightest bit bothered?		
4. If you saw your boyfriend/girl-friend not looking as attractive as usual, would you	a) make a comment to show your disapproval? b) feel disappointed that he/she wasn't as good-looking as you thought? c) hardly notice the difference?		
5. When you get dressed up to go out, do you	a) wear things to please yourself? b) wear things to please your boy or girlfriend? c) wear things to make your friends feel a bit envious?		
6. Do you think that girls who have hairy legs should shave them?	a) Yes b) No c) Not bothered one way or the other.		
7. Do you think it looks funny if boys are shorter than their girlfriends?	a) Yes b) No c) Never notice		
8. If you get a crop of spots on your face, do you	a) try to disguise them with make-up or cream? b) feel very self-conscious and try to avoid people till they're gone? c) never let them worry you?		
9. Do you mind going out with someone who isn't very good looking?	a) Yes b) No c) Only if there's no alternative		
10. Do you envy friends who always seem to have more fashionable clothes than you?	a) Often b) Sometimes c) Never		

VERDICT

10 — 20 You could be a real 'sucker' for the ad-man! Very likely to believe that what is important in life is good looks and nice clothes. You might be in danger of not valuing people for what they really are and being more concerned with outward appearances. Watch out! You're in danger of being a teenage puppet with the ad-man pulling the strings!

20 — 30 You're not so likely to judge yourself and others purely by outward appearances and possessions but you are in danger of believing that if you're not good-looking, fashionably dressed and popular with the opposite sex, then you're a social failure. Remember that people have other qualities and it's better to be an individual than a slavish follower of trends dictated by the ad-man.

30 — 34 If you're being honest, you don't seem to be very worried by what the ad-man and your friends think is fashionable and trendy. You've got a mind of your own. You don't only judge people by their outward appearances and you're quite likely to be more appreciative of their other qualities. So long as your answers don't mean that you're totally insensitive to other people and what they think about you, then you sound like a real individual. The ad-man will have a hard job influencing you.

1 Discuss your scores together.
   a) Do you agree with verdict on your score? Give your reasons.
   b) Compare the verdicts on boys and girls in your class.
   c) Is either sex more likely to be influenced by the ad-man in matters of dress and personal appearance? Which? Can you suggest any reasons for this?

2 Make a collection of adverts from magazines and newspapers that are particularly directed at young people.
   a) What kind of feelings and emotions is each advert designed to appeal to?
   b) What percentage of the adverts are directed at girls; boys; both sexes?
   c) Give examples from your collection of adverts which use sex to sell their products.
   d) What are the qualities of an 'ideal teenager' according to the adverts?

3 Which adverts do you think have most influence on young people and adults, those in newspapers and magazines or those on television? Give as many reasons as you can to support your answer.

4 Give examples of television adverts which
   a) use sex to draw attention to their products.
   b use humour to draw attention to their products.
   c) use repetition, a catch phrase or a special jingle to draw attention to their products.
   d) use animals or cute children to draw attention to their products.

5 Give examples of television adverts which try to impress the public by 'scientific research'. What's the danger of believing these 'research findings' without question?

6 Do you think that the general public is impressed by 'ordinary people' in adverts who prove that one washing powder is better than another or that they can't tell the difference between a certain margarine and butter? Why?

7 Do you think the public is more likely to buy a product if it's advertised by a well-known film star or sporting personality? Why?

8. Describe in words and pictures 'an ideal Mum' and 'a successful man with the ladies' according to the adverts. What view of men and women and the relationship between them do these adverts display?

9. Produce adverts of your own to advertise 'Spots Off' skin cream for teenagers, 'Umbridge' medicine, 'Ripp-off' cigars and 'Weezy-Oozie' washing powder. You can either produce them as drawings for magazines or as a playlet for television.

NEIL AND PETER

'FATTY' TAUNTS DRIVE BOY, 14, TO STARVATION.

A boy almost starved himself to death after 'fatty' insults by boys at his school.

The boy, Neil Ward, aged 14, slimmed from twelve stone to six before being rushed to a city's psychiatric hospital when doctors feared for his life.

Now his mother claims her son is in a ward surrounded by drug addicts, psychopaths and highly disturbed patients.

And she fears the experience could scar her son for life.

Hospital authorities, concerned by the case, say there is nowhere else for Neil to go in Sheffield.

He was given a cubicle in a mixed open ward at the city's Middlewood Hospital last week when doctors believed he would die.

Neil — so weak he could not walk — was suffering from the slimming disease, anorexia nervosa.

Liquid

The boy, who at times went three weeks without a meal, is recovering after taking a little liquid food. BUT the danger of the stay in Ward 18 yesterday left his mother, housewife Mrs Joan Ward, aged 40, 'very upset and very concerned'.

Mrs Ward, of Clifton Crescent North, Rotherham, Yorks, said: 'There are drug addicts and psychopaths in the ward, many of them extremely depressed. I know it is extremely upsetting for my son.

'The doctors and staff have been wonderful. But I just don't think it is right to have a boy of 14 in a ward like that.

'I would plead with him, but he just wasn't interested. He said he didn't want to eat, it would make him fat.'

A spokesman for the hospital said: 'Neil is in a cubicle of his own but we have no facilities to treat and care emotionally disturbed adolescents.'

PROBLEM

Neil's case is obviously a fairly extreme reaction to being taunted by his friends. Not many teenagers would be driven to such desperate lengths to become accepted by other young people. But being made fun of by other teenagers is something we all experience at times. And for some of us, if it happens a lot, then it can be a very painful experience.

Sometimes it's very hard to be an individual and to be able to withstand the pressure to be like everyone else. Some teenagers try to appear big in the eyes of their friends by making fun of or looking down on others. Presumably they don't think about the harmful effects of their behaviour.

AN INQUIRY

Set up an inquiry into the case of a boy like Neil. Let's call him Peter. Give individual pupils roles to play. You will have to present your arguments very clearly and really try to show how the people involved must have felt. Put yourself in their place and try to act as they would have done. Those not playing key roles can be members of the audience, anxious to ask questions and to decide which is the most likely explanation for the sad course of events which led to Peter's confinement in hospital.

THINGS TO FIND OUT

Before you begin it's important to sort out one or two facts which should be taken into account in the inquiry.

1   What are the causes and symptoms of the disease *anorexia nervosa*?
2   Do many young people suffer from this disease?
3   Could the insults from friends be enough in themselves to make the boy ill?
4   What is a psychiatric hospital? Why should he have been sent to one?
5   Can you find any evidence or give other examples of teenagers being seriously upset by the bullying or teasing of their friends?

ROLES

The Chairman/Chairwoman.   You are responsible for organizing the inquiry, calling on the various witnesses, asking the audience for questions and trying to arrive at some kind of explanation of the case.

Mrs Joan Mitchell, Peter's mother.   You are very upset by Peter's illness and feel ashamed that he is in a psychiatric hospital. You don't want to admit that he is 'emotionally disturbed'.

Mr Mitchell, Peter's father.   You got very angry with your son when he wouldn't eat and even tried to force him against his will. You now feel very bitter that the school did nothing to protect him from the insults of the other pupils.

Elsie Farrow, Peter's married sister.   You say that originally Peter used to eat a lot because he was unhappy — almost for compensation. But then the taunts at school made him even more unhappy and so he refused to eat at all. You think that your parents might have been a bit to blame for not helping him earlier.

James Bowen, Peter's Headmaster.   You're the Head of a large school and Peter's case didn't come to your attention until too late.

Bill Scott, Peter's Games Master.   You were pleased when he began to lose weight. He hated Games and often truanted from your lessons. You had told him he was overweight.

Mary Field, Peter's Form Teacher.   You had constantly tried to protect Peter from other pupils in the class who made fun of him and called him 'fatty'. You said it was just 'puppy fat' and that he'd grow out of it.

Margaret Finch, School Counsellor.   You're responsible for dealing with pupils with personal problems. Peter was constantly being reported to you for missing lessons, 'attention-seeking' in class and 'disruptive behaviour'. You think all this had something to do with his weight.

Dr Maureen Brown, doctor at the hospital.   You explain why Peter needs to be in a psychiatric hospital.

Dr David Ross, doctor at the hospital.   You're an expert on teenage emotional problems. You explain what kinds of pressures from friends and society generally can make some young people like Peter become ill.

Chris Evans
Steve Russel
Tony Boston
Gail Newman
Susan Jones
Rick Harding
    You're all pupils from Peter's class. Some of you were responsible for teasing him. Others deny any responsibility. Some now feel very guilty and want to make amends.

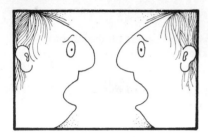

1

Imagine you are a candidate for the 'Teenage Party' in government elections. Make a speech to the electors about what measures you would introduce to make things better for British teenagers.

2

'Teenage magazines are all the same.' 'When you've read one you've read them all.' 'Why don't girls get bored with the same old drivel about puny pop stars and sloppy romance stories week after week?' Make out an argument to either criticize or defend girls' magazines.

3

If you believed everything you read in the press, you'd think that all teenagers were scruffy, long-haired, dope-taking vandals! It's unfair to judge everyone by the behaviour and appearance of a few.
Pretend you are a newspaper reporter and explain why you often describe teenagers in this way.

4

'A girl is usually looking for a steady boyfriend whom she can imagine marrying — a boy is more concerned with sex.'
You've probably heard this said before. But when pupils in a Leeds school were asked for their opinions, half the boys and a third of the girls disagreed with the statement. What's your opinion? Give as many reasons as you can to support your view.

1 Explain the difference between the 'age of consent' and the 'age of majority'.
2 At what age can you marry with our parents' consent?
3 At what age can you vote?
4 Which teenagers, according to Murdock and Phelps, are most interested in pop?
5 What else are young people most interested in according to Murdock and Phelps?
6 Name three of the 'unseen faces' behind successful pop groups.
7 Which street in London became associated with Mod fashions in the sixties?
8 What were the two main criticisms of America made by the Hippy movement?
9 Which rock operas helped to popularize Christianity with teenagers in the early 70s?
10 What are the causes and symptoms of *anorexia nervosa?*

It's often the bad things that teenagers do which attracts all the publicity. We don't hear so much about the good things. But teenagers are the most energetic age-group there is when it comes to raising money for charity. Sponsored walks, non-stop dancing, jumble-sales, concerts and competitions are among the most common ways of raising money. But a quick look at *The Guinness Book of Records* will show you that some people have done, more original and amusing things to get publicity. And quite often the publicity has been tied in with a fund-raising event of some kind.

You will come across several organizations in this book who depend on charity to continue with their work. There are hundreds of others who try to make the world a better place for those who are underprivileged in some way. In an ideal society, the underprivileged wouldn't exist. Or the State would be more responsible for people in need. But such a time is a long way off and in the meantime people need help now.

Choose one or more organizations whose work you approve of and plan a way of raising money to help them. Get some help from your teacher in putting the plan into action.

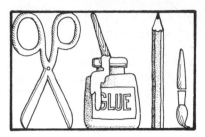

1

Conduct a survey to find out which teenage magazines are most popular in your school. What features do teenagers look for in a good magazine?

Dear Aunt Jane,

My boyfriend and I have been going out for 3 years and last night.....

2

Make a collection of the 'Problem Pages' from girls' magazines. What kind of problems do the writers most often describe? How serious and how genuine are they? What kind of advice is given? How useful and genuine is it?

3

A doctor writing about our over-use of drugs said recently, 'The number of pills swallowed each year in Britain would fill the Albert Hall! If you shook some people they'd rattle.'
He was referring mostly to adults and not teenagers. Yet drug-addiction is usually thought to be a teenage problem.
Make a study of the different types of drugs taken by young people and adults, their uses and misuses.

ROYAL ALBERT HALL

4

Legally teenagers can't buy cigarettes for their own use until sixteen or drinks in a pub until eighteen. And yet many do. Make a study of the smoking and drinking habits of your class mates. What reasons do they give for their behaviour?

5

In 1973 the number of illegitimate births to girls under nineteen was around 60 000. Fifty-six per cent of the babies born to mothers under twenty were conceived before they got married.

Abortions for the same age group passed 70.000. Nearly all of these could have been prevented by contraception.

Make a study of the different methods of contraception. Which are the most reliable? Are any methods dangerous to health?

What is the attitude of the medical and religious authorities to contraception?

6

How have teenagers' lives changed over the years? Make a comparison in words and pictures of the work and leisure activities of teenagers in the 1870s, the 1930s and the present day.

7

What makes a good youth club? Imagine you have the responsibility for setting up and running a club for teenagers you know. How would you go about it? What activities would you include? What problems would you expect? How would you overcome them?

Include information from interviews with teenagers, parents, teachers, social workers, the police, and people who already run Youth Clubs. How far do you agree with their ideas?

Would you be more careful if it was you that got pregnant?

Contraception is one of the facts of life.
Anyone married or single can get advice on contraception from the Family Planning Association.
Margaret Pyke House, 25-35 Mortimer Street, London W1 N 8BQ. Tel. 01-636 9135.

6 FAMILY MATTERS

FAMILY STRUCTURE

NUCLEAR FAMILIES

Before the Second World War most working-class people lived with, or very near to their relatives. It was quite common to find elderly parents living with their married children, and newly-weds sharing a house with their in-laws until they could find somewhere of their own. People often lived in the same street or round the corner from their relatives. They saw each other every day and shared their good fortune and their troubles. Family ties were close and strong.

Middle-class family life had already begun to change before the war. From the beginning of the century middle-class parents had started the trend of having fewer children. As the century wore on, they began to realize that, if you wanted to be able to afford to bring up children well, if you didn't want to spend all your life in child-birth and child-rearing, and if women were to have careers, too — then it was better to have two or three children instead of five or six.

Improved methods of contraception made it possible for them to limit their family size.

Middle-class people found it easier to rent or buy their own houses. They were more likely to move to different parts of the country from where they started, to live and work. And as they earned more money, a sign of their success was to move to better homes in the suburbs.

Today most people (but not all) from both middle-class and working-class backgrounds have adopted this kind of family life. The typical family group today is mother, father and two or three children living on their own in a small or medium-sized house, or in a flat, usually quite far away from other relatives. Sometimes an old parent lives with them but often there is no room. Elderly people are more likely to live by themselves these days or in an old people's home. Relatives might only be seen two or three times a year instead of two or three times a week.

This type of family group is called a NUCLEAR FAMILY.

EXTENDED FAMILIES

In India and Pakistan parents, children and grand-parents, married sons and daughters, cousins and aunts and uncles, even great-grandparents, are all part of one big family group. Family life in the villages may mean as many as a hundred people living under the same roof. No child or elderly person ever needs to feel neglected and the duties and responsibilities of daily life are carried out together for the benefit of all.

This type of living arrangement, with different generations and relatives living closely together, is called an EXTENDED FAMILY or a JOINT FAMILY.

Asian families in Britain may be smaller than in the village communities at home but the same principles of living together, sharing work, food and income, looking after children, caring for the elderly and sick, arranging marriages, celebrating religious ceremonies and sorting out problems is still typical.

Duties and responsibilities are more bound up with religion and customs than in British families. And individuals who go against them or bring shame on the family, risk losing all contact for ever after with their relatives and next of kin. Most would rather die than experience such a fate! When the rules of family life are so strict, and when duty means so much, it's small wonder that Indians and Pakistanis are often critical of nuclear families in Britain.

A LOOK AT BOTH

1 Middle-class families started the trend towards nuclear families before the working class. In the period before the Second World War, how would you have recognized middle-class people compared to working-class people? How would their houses, jobs, dress, leisure activities and attitudes differ do you think? Are there the same differences between middle-class and working-class people today? Give as many illustrations as you can to support your answer.

2 Some British families can still be called EXTENDED FAMILIES. Perhaps you're part of one yourself. Mrs Knock certainly is.

'Mrs Knock, aged 64, lives with her husband, a single son and a grand-daughter of 6 years old. Her eldest daughter lives in the next street and her youngest daughter in the same street. She sees them and their children every day. They help her with the shopping and she looks after the grand-children when they are at work. They even pay her a little for doing it. Her youngest son, recently married, lives two streets away and calls every evening. Her two daughters have the midday meal with her and she sends a meal to her youngest son because his wife is at work during the day'. (From *The Family Life of Old People*, by Peter Townsend)

a) How does the life of an extended family in Britain differ from that of a nuclear family?

b) What are the advantages and disadvantages of living in an extended family in your opinion?

c) What are the advantages and disadvantages of living in a nuclear family in your opinion? Give examples to illustrate your answer.

3 Why do some Indian and Pakistani settlers in Britain often criticize the nuclear family? Do you agree that members of a nuclear family take their duties and responsibilities to relatives less seriously than members of an extended family? Give full reasons for your answer.

*4 Indian and Pakistani settlers in Britain are either Moslems, Hindus or Sikhs.
Find out the attitudes of each of these religions to
a) authority in the family
b) marriage and divorce
c) contraception
d) care of the elderly
d) the role of women

*5 Give two or three examples of the kind of behaviour which is said 'to bring shame' on Indian and Pakistani families.

*6 What are the special responsibilities of elderly people, the eldest son and women in the Asian extended family?

*7 Find examples of other societies in which people live in extended families.

*8 'You fall in love, marry and repent at leisure,' says the Asian. 'We marry and then fall in love. Then there is less chance of disillusion.'
a) Explain how parents go about arranging marriages for their children.
b) What factors do they take into consideration?
c) Why does the system seem to work so well in India and Pakistan but often cause conflicts between parents and their children when they move to Britain?

*9 Find out about the different customs and ceremonies of Sikhs, Moslems and Hindus when they are celebrating births and marriages and mourning deaths. Compare them with similar ceremonies in Britain.
a) Describe the religious festivals of Holi, Ganesh Chaturthi and Ramadan.
b) Describe the Christian festivals of Christmas and Easter and the Jewish celebration of Passover.

*For extra information and ideas write to:
The Community Relations Commission, 15-16 Bedford Street, London WC2E 9HY.

KEEPING UP WITH THE JONESES

Families in Britain are great CONSUMERS. They buy the food, clothes and manufactured goods of all kinds which industries want to sell. Each year their demands increase and industries compete with each other to satisfy them.

In the middle are the advertising men whose job it is to give publicity to various products. Clever ad-men can persuade people to buy things they don't need and to want things they see advertised. One of the reasons why families in Britain consume more and more each year is because advertising men have done their job so well.

Look carefully at this picture and make a list of the goods and equipment which the Jones family have been encouraged to buy.

1 In your list of goods bought by the Joneses, which of them are:
   a) absolutely necessary?
   b) nice to have if you can afford them?
   c) unnecessary and could be done without?

2 Which of them
   a) help to make life easier?
   b) help to make life pleasanter?
   c) could be given up without being missed very much?

3 Draw a picture of your own to illustrate the outside of the Joneses house and garden marking in some of the CONSUMER GOODS you might expect to find there. Which of them are
   a) absolutely necessary?
   b) nice if you can afford them?
   c) unnecessary and could be done without?

4 The Joneses were the first family in their street to get a colour television. Now the neighbours on both sides have bought colour televisions. Give examples of household possessions which are sometimes thought to be 'status symbols' by those who own them. Give examples of the ways in which advertising men often encourage people to 'keep up with the Joneses' as a way of selling products.

5 Which groups of consumers do you think are most likely to buy the biggest number of household goods:
   a) single people living alone?
   b) nuclear families in their own or rented houses?
   c) extended families living a fairly close and shared way of life?
   Give full reasons for your answers.

6 Families also 'consume' the leisure activities, services and entertainments provided by commercially run businesses, e.g. holidays, clubs, restaurants and cinemas.
   a) Give examples of what are sometimes described as SERVICE INDUSTRIES.
   b) Make a list of commercially organized social activities and entertainments.
   c) In your grandparents' day families used to make the most of their own entertainments. Suggest reasons why commercially organized activities have steadily increased during the last thirty years or so.

THE AD·MAN'S FAMILY

Make a list of television commercials which use a family setting as part of the advert. Choose any three and describe in detail what you notice about them.

a) Who is the main character in the advert?
b) How is the wife/mother portrayed?
   What are the main characteristics of advert-mums? Are they true to life? Give examples to illustrate your description.
c) How is the father/husband portrayed?
   What are the main characteristics of advert-husbands? Are they true to life? Give examples to illustrate your description.
d) How are the children portrayed?
   Suggest why children are portrayed in this way. Are they true to life?
e) Apart from the product being advertised, what attitudes to family life is the advert encouraging?
f) What particular emotions is the advert appealing to?

MASCULINE - FEMININE: WHAT'S THE DIFFERENCE ?

Despite what our friends say, most people have fairly fixed ideas about what they think is masculine and feminine behaviour. Find out what the average man and woman in the street thinks by asking a sample of twenty people (ten men and ten women) to answer these questions. (You will need to duplicate at least twenty copies of this questionnaire.)

WITH ALL THIS UNISEX BUSINESS I CAN'T TELL WHICH IS WHICH THESE DAYS!

	MEN	WOMEN	EITHER SEX
1 Here are a list of human qualities. Put those you think are characteristic of men in the column marked 'men', those characteristic of women in the column marked 'women', and those characteristic of either in the column marked 'either sex'. Bravery, compassion, gentleness, jealousy, nosiness, cattiness, pride, strength, clear thinking, independence, loyalty, self-sacrifice, reliability, weakness, responsibility, aggression.			

	AGREE	DIS-AGREE	DON'T KNOW
2 Put a tick in column 1 or 2 depending on whether you agree or disagree with the following statements. If you don't know put a tick in column 3. a) It's natural for women to do the housework and bring up the children. b) It's natural for men to be the bread-winners. c) It's natural for women to be more concerned about their appearance than men. d) It's unnatural for men to spend a lot of time looking after small children. f) It's unnatural for women to be the bosses in charge of men.			

3 Please complete these sentences in your own words:
   I think being feminine means ....
   I think being masculine means ....
Thank you for answering these questions.

When twenty people have completed your questionnaire, use the information they gave to answer the following questions:

1 Compare all the replies to question 1. Which three qualities were most often said to be characteristic of a) men, b) women, and c) either sex?

2 Add up all the replies to the statements in question 2. In each case say how many people a) agreed, b) disagreed, or c) didn't know what to think, about the statement. Write a short paragraph to describe what most people in your sample thought was 'natural' and 'unnatural' behaviour for men and women.

3 Using their answers to question 3, write a short paragraph to describe the ways in which most people in your sample defined 'masculinity' and 'femininity'.

By now you should have some idea what the general public think about masculinity and femininity. But remember these are only their OPINIONS. And opinions can be based on prejudice and faulty information.

MASCULINE – FEMININE STEREOTYPES

Although each individual is different to some extent, we still tend to think that men should behave in one way and women in another. We expect men and women to have different qualities and temperaments. And we could all give two or three examples of their typical strengths and weaknesses.

These fixed ideas about the sort of characteristics that belong to men and women are called STEREOTYPES. But stereotypes can be misleading. Think of the stereotype that many people have of teenagers — that 'teenagers are all long-haired, drug-taking, sex-mad vandals' who 'don't know they're born these days' and 'get things too easy'. No doubt you've heard this kind of view before. It's arrived at by picking on the characteristics of one or two teenagers, exaggerating them wildly and then applying them to all young people.

Many of our stereotyped ideas about what is 'typically masculine' and 'typically feminine' behaviour are equally exaggerated and inaccurate.

Stop and think for a minute about some of the things that are said about men and women.

'Women are the weaker sex.'

'Every woman needs a man to look after her.'

'Women make terrible drivers.'

'Women aren't mechanically minded.'

'Men are like little boys. They never grow up.'

'Women are too soft. They always get weepy when things go wrong.'

'Men are useless in the kitchen.'

'You can rely on a man to get things done.'

'The man is the head of the house. He's the breadwinner, he's the boss and he makes the big decisions.'

Are these characteristics true of all men and women? Surely not. Some women may make terrible drivers. But then, so do some men. Some men are useless in the kitchen because they've never had to learn how to cook. But many are not, and some expert cooks are men.

For each of these so-called 'typical characteristics' of men and women, you could probably give examples of people you know who don't fit the bill at all. Are your examples just exceptions to the rule? Or is the rule a bit out of date?

1 Draw a series of cartoons of your own to show how the stereotyped things said about men and women in our society are often inaccurate or out of date. For example . . .

'Men don't get worked up and emotional about things.'

2 Nowadays there are plenty of male pop stars and their teenage followers who wear flimsy clothes, jewellery, high-heeled shoes and make-up — in fact all the things which were once thought to be signs of femininity. Fashions and attitudes are obviously changing. Can you give any other examples of ways in which our opinions about masculinity and femininity have changed in recent years?

DO HUSBANDS MAKE GOOD HOUSEWIVES ?

With forty per cent of married women going out to work these days, it's obvious that 'a woman's place' is no longer 'in the home'. What usually happens now is that women work until they have children and then go back to work when their children are old enough to go to school. For some, this means doing two jobs, worker and housewife. The increasing equality between the sexes in our society means that men's lives have to alter too.

The 1971 census reported that more than one million men who stayed at home described their occupation as 'housewife', and that one in five women earned more than their husbands.

Helping in the home comes easier to some men than others. Many still think it's degrading for a man to be seen cleaning up, changing nappies or ironing clothes. But this is what sharing the housework means. Washing the odd pot and reading a bed-time story to the children isn't much in comparison to all the other things that have to be done.

Ann Oakley* wanted to find out just how much men were prepared to do, how much their wives would let them do and what both sides felt about their changing roles. So she interviewed some married couples in London.

She found that men would rather help with the children than the household chores. One wife explained, 'He plays a lot with the children while I'm washing up and keeps them quiet and sometimes

* 'Are Husbands Good Housewives?' Ann Oakley (*New Society*)

he'll help me to bath them and put them to bed.' But most men drew the line at changing nappies. One wife said, 'If I'm changing a nappy he runs out of the room. It makes him sick. He thinks it's my duty.'

What about housework? Ann Oakley found that the husbands she interviewed did the washing up and made the tea occasionally. Most of them agreed with the wife who said, 'I don't agree with men doing housework. I don't think it's a man's job. I certainly wouldn't like to see my husband cleaning a room up. I don't think it's mannish. . . . I like a man to be a man.'

To put it simply, the men seemed to avoid all but the enjoyable aspects of being with children. Very few got involved in the physical side of housework, and few women expected them to.

From the men's point of view it's easy to see how 'playing with children' can be a nice addition to their role. It's a pleasant activity; washing nappies is not. In fact the women seemed to gain nothing from the changes in their husbands' roles except some temporary peace and quiet in which to get on with the household chores. They had lost some of their more pleasant responsibilities and kept all the unpleasant ones!

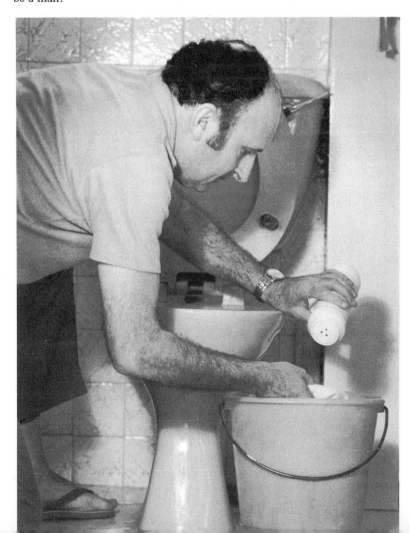

	COUPLE	1	2	3	4	5	6	7	8	9	10
BACKGROUND DETAILS	wife not working										
	wife working (full-time)	✓									
	wife working (part time)		✓								
	age group										
	20-30		✓								
	30-40	✓									
	40-50										
	50-60+										
	children under 5		✓								
	washing up										
	cleaning floors										
	washing clothes										
	ironing										
	shopping										
	cooking										
	changing nappies										
	bathing baby										
	pushing pram										
	playing with children										

When you've interviewed ten couples, discuss your findings together with your teacher.

1 a) Which household jobs did husbands help with most often and which jobs did they never do?

   b) Were husbands with working wives more likely to share the housework than those with wives who stayed at home?

   c) Which age group of husbands were most likely to help with housework?

   d) When the couples had young children, did husbands help both with the housework and the children; help only with the housework; help only with the children; not help very much with either?

   e) From the ten couples you interviewed and the star ratings you gave the husbands, how many shared the housework and looking after the children equally with their wives; let their wives do most of the housework but helped them out from time to time; let their wives do all the housework?

2 How often have you heard women say this about their husbands? Or husband 'plead ignorance' as a way of avoiding cooking, sewing or ironing? It's true that girls have often had to learn these things in childhood and boys haven't. Explain how you would bring up children of your own so that they could take a more equal share in household chores when they get married.

3 Interview some men and women you know about their attitudes to changes in the roles of men and women.

   a) Do they still think 'a woman's place is in the home' and a man is degraded by housework? Or do they think that men and women should take more of an equal share in household tasks these days?

   b) What's your opinion? Give as many reasons as you can to support your views.

4 Ann Oakley found that for her couples, things hadn't changed very much. If anything, women had lost some of the more pleasant aspects of their responsibilities and kept only the unpleasant ones. Suggest reasons why the men tended to avoid unpleasant jobs. Do you think this is fair? Why?

5 What other jobs around the house should girls learn how to do if equality is going to work both ways?

I THINK IT WORKS BOTH WAYS – IT'S NO USE A WOMAN TELLING ME TO SEW ON A BUTTON IF SHE CAN'T MEND A FUSE!

6 Make out a time-sheet for some housewives you know, showing all the days of the week and the list of jobs they have to do. Mark in how many hours per day they usually spend on these tasks. And then add up the total for the week. How many hours per week do your housewives spend doing household jobs? Is it more or less than the average hours worked each week by men at work (see p.26).

HE WOULD HELP ME MORE IF I LET HIM, BUT HE'S SO USELESS. IT'S QUICKER TO DO THE JOB MYSELF!

MEN'S JOBS AND WOMEN'S JOBS

Eight out of ten women who go out to work in Great Britain are employed in one of four types of jobs:

Office and clerical work	30.3%
Catering and domestic services	20.4%
Unskilled and semi-skilled factory work	15.9%
Shop work	10.1%
Total	76.7%

This means that some jobs have come to be thought of as 'women's jobs'. For example:

Jobs in which over 90% of the workers are women

typist   *canteen assistant*   *sewing machinist*   *nurse*   *maid*

Jobs in which 75% – 90% of the workers are women

shop assistant   *telephone operator*   *cleaner*   *hairdresser*

   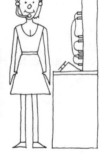  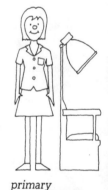

Jobs in which 60% – 75% of the workers are women

cashier   *packer*   *cook*   *primary school teacher*

Other jobs are usually thought of as 'men's jobs'.
For example:

Jobs in which over 90% of the workers are men

engineer

police officer

armed forces

car mechanic

building labourer

construction worker

commercial traveller

miner

driver

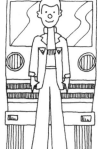

postman

manager

Jobs which require qualifications and training or which give power, influence, or prestige to the people who do them are sometimes called 'top jobs'. The number of women doing 'top jobs' compared to men is small as these figures for 1971 show.

Percentage of men and women in top jobs in Great Britain 1971

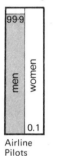 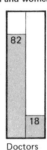  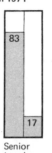  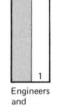  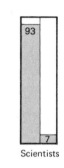

Airline Pilots	Doctors	Senior Civil Servants and MPs	Senior Local Government officers	Lawyers and Solicitors	Engineers and Technologists	Accountants and Company Secretaries	Scientists
men 99·9 / women 0.1	82 / 18	89 / 11	83 / 17	96 / 4	99 / 1	83 / 17	93 / 7

In Russia, on the other hand, not only do women navvies tear up the roads with pneumatic drills and provide one third of the labour force on building sites, but they also do more of the 'top jobs' than women in Britain. For example,

Doctors:	75% are women
Scientists:	38% are women
Engineers:	32% are women
Lawyers:	43% are women

1 Some jobs are done mainly by men and some mainly by women. Do you think the reasons for this are
  a) biological?
  b) practical?
  c) financial?
  d) because of tradition?
  e) because of stereotyped ideas about the characteristics of men and women?
  Give full reasons for your answer.

2 Explain fully why some jobs are called 'top jobs'. Why are the jobs in the chart above called 'top jobs'?

3 Suggest reasons why so few women in Britain do these jobs. Describe some of the problems which women wanting to do these jobs have to overcome.

4 Find out what facilities are provided in countries like Russia to help women have more of a share of the 'top jobs'.

5 Arrange with your teacher for men and women doing 'untypical' jobs to come and talk to you about them (e.g. a woman mechanic, politician, police officer, or doctor; a male nurse, cook or hairdresser). Find out why they chose their jobs, whether they experienced any prejudice from people who thought they were the 'wrong sex for the job', and if they find their jobs interesting and worthwhile.

6. At midnight on 28 December 1975 important legislation was introduced in Britain. The Equal Pay Act finally became law and the Sex Discrimination Act made it illegal to differentiate between men and women in work, leisure and educational opportunities. A Special Equal Opportunities Commission was set up to hear complaints about DISCRIMINATION and to make recommendations to the Government about future changes in the law.

  a) What were the main changes brought about by the Equal Pay Act?
  b) Why did the Act do very little to help women in low-paid jobs?
  c) How did some employers try to avoid giving women equal pay with men?
  d) What changes did the Sex Discrimination Act bring about in relation to adverts for jobs and job appointments?
  e) Which jobs are still kept for men only and women only by law?
  f) Even though most jobs are now legally open to both men and women, why are jobs like those on pp.92-93 still done mainly by men or mainly by women?
  g) What are the two main responsibilities of the Equal Opportunities Commission?
  h) Can you give any examples of men or women who have been helped by the Equal Opportunities Commission?

OLD AND ALONE

Mrs Cooper is typical of many old people who are housebound because of illness. She gets help from the Social Services, visitors call to see her and her pension is just about enough to live on with the extra money she gets from her son. But her life has lost its meaning and one day follows the other in dreary monotony. Compared to many old people she isn't particularly neglected. There are thousands who are much worse off.

Mrs Cooper is sixty-nine. Three years ago she had a stroke which left her partially paralysed down the left side. This means she can't get out and about without help.

Her husband died six years ago. She has a married son living in the south of England who comes to see her when he can. She's lived in her present house in Birmingham for twenty-five years and for this reason doesn't want to move south or into an old people's home.

She gets more visitors than a lot of old people: a neighbour from down the street, some school children from the local comprehensive, the vicar's wife and an old work-mate she's known since before the war.

A home help comes each day for about an hour and sometimes stays longer to chat to Mrs Cooper when her work is done.

A typical day in her life begins at 6 a.m. when she wakes up and switches on the radio at the side of her bed. She lies in bed listening to it for about an hour before struggling to get up. It takes her a long time to get dressed because she can only use one arm.

Breakfast consists of tea and bread and jam. She looks at the newspaper through spectacles long needing to be replaced. When the home help arrives she makes the bed, tidies up and does the shopping. Mrs Cooper sits by the window looking out until its time for the television programmes to begin. Her whole life seems to revolve around the television and she peers continually at the clock to see if it's time to switch on. Sometimes she even watches the test-card because the background music is better than the silence of an empty house.

For lunch she eats sandwiches left by the home help and for tea some cold meat or cheese. Her paralysis makes cooking difficult and she's afraid to use the gas stove in case she sets light to herself.

Her movements are unsteady and she frequently falls. Besides the cuts and bruises and the damage to ornaments and furniture, the falls have shaken her confidence. Each day she makes less and less effort to get about. Once she fell down in the evening and hadn't the strength to pull herself up again until the home help arrived next morning.

She goes to bed at about 8 p.m. after another long struggle to get undressed.

Her constant companion is a black cat which looks almost as old as she. Sometimes it lies lazily on her knee, takes very little exercise and eats any of the leftovers she chooses to give it. She often talks to it but it's too old even to notice.

Last week a social worker visited Mrs Cooper to see what could be done to help.

Soccer-Mad Gran Cops a Ban

Granny Alice Dakin has been branded Britain's oldest soccer rowdy.

The football-crazy grandmother has been banned from the ground of the team she has supported for thirty-five years.

The order came after 60-year-old Alice was involved in stormy scenes at the end of the match.

A player was hit in the mouth and a linesman was clouted with a supporter's rattle.

Officials of Southern League Stourbridge Town decided that Alice would have to go after they were ordered to face a Football Association inquiry into their fans' 'unruly behaviour'.

Improvements in science and medicine, more nourishing food and a higher standard of living have all helped to prolong human life. As a result the number of elderly people in Britain today is almost nine million — roughly sixteen percent of the population.

These old people, who in their lifetime have brought up families, worked hard, and perhaps made important contributions to society, are described today by all kinds of influential people — sociologists, doctors, social workers, politicians — as a problem. It seems as though the only time we hear about old people on the television or read about them in the news-papers is when 'the problems of old age' are being discussed.

But is it fair to stereotype all old people in this way? After all, Churchill didn't take on the job of war-time prime minister until he was sixty-five. Picasso was still painting pictures at ninety. Jack Warner still acted the part of Sergeant Dixon of Dock Green at seventy. Arthur Askey is still going strong at over seventy-five.

Old age isn't seen to be a problem in all societies. In China for example, the role of the elderly is very important. They are greatly respected for their wisdom and experience. They play an important part in running the house and looking after children while mothers and fathers are at work. The same is true in India and Pakistan. No one would dream of leaving old relatives to fend for themselves or of not consulting them when important decisions have to be made.

Why, then, in our society are the elderly considered to be a problem? And what do we mean by the term? Granny Dakin certainly caused a bit of trouble to Stourbridge Town football club. Is she an example of the kind of problem experts are talking about?

1 For Mrs Cooper, life has lost its meaning. Suggest
a) how her house could be adapted to make things more convenient for her.
b) how she could be encouraged to take more exercise and get out and about a little more.
2 Arrange with your teacher for a social worker to come and tell you about his/her job.
a) What contacts does he/she have with elderly people?
b) What particular problems do they have?
c) What can social workers and the local authority do to help?
d) What proportion of elderly people in your village, town or city live alone; live with their husband or wife; live with relatives; live in an old people's home?

For extra information write to:

Age Concern,
Bernard Sunley House,
60, Pitcairn Road,
Mitcham,
Surrey.

Help the Aged,
8, Denman Street,
London, W.1.

3 Who's Who? Make a collection of life histories of elderly people you know. Include both famous old people and your relatives and neighbours. Show how many old people still lead a lively and interesting life and make a real contribution to those around them or to society generally. Include photographs, taped interviews and details of their early life wherever you can.

GERIATRIC WARD

Feeding time in the geriatric ward;
I wondered how they found their mouths,
and seeing that not one looked up, inquired
'Do they have souls?'

'If I had a machine-gun,' answered the doctor,
'I'd show you dignity in death instead of living death.
Death wasn't meant to be kept alive.
But we're under orders
to pump blood and air in after the mind's gone.
I don't understand souls;
I only learned about cells
law-abiding as leaves
withering under frost.
But we, never handing over
to Mother who knows best,
spray cabbages with oxygen,
        hoping for a smile,
count pulses of breathing bags
        whose direction is lost,
and think we've won.

Here's a game you can't win —
One by one they ooze away in the cold.
There's no society forbidding
this dragged -out detention of the old.'

Phoebe Hesketh

Read and discuss this poem together. Describe exactly what's wrong with the old people in the geriatric ward. What's the doctor's attitude?

Some people argue that when old folk are senile, when babies are born severely mentally or physically deformed and when people have incurable diseases, they should be 'helped to die'. The official term is EUTHANASIA or 'mercy killing'.

Some doctors do practise mercy killing already, but officially the practice is illegal and doctors who do it can be convicted of manslaughter.

There are all kinds of arguments about why it should be kept illegal and just as many on the other side from those who feel it's more humane to put people out of their misery.

Before giving your own opinion, question doctors, lawyers and representatives of different religions about their attitudes to euthanasia. What are the arguments for and against? Discuss them together. Can you find any accounts from people who have witnessed mercy-killing, or who have seen some of the distressing effects of keeping very ill or very senile people alive?

When you have considered all points of view, make a speech giving your own views on whether euthanasia should or should not be made legal.

FAMILY LIFE IN CHINA

China before 1949

China is a country which few people in Britain know much about. Yet it is one of the biggest in the world. It has a population of about 800 000 000 — a quarter of the world's total population.

For thousands of years the people of China lived a hard life. Power and wealth belonged to a few landowners, while the great majority of the population lived in extreme poverty. This peasant poem describes what life was like:

We have only worn-out straw huts to live in.
Every day we can only afford a cup of rotten vegetables,
In front of our houses are piles of rubbish.
Behind our houses there are stinking ponds.
During the day everywhere is full of flies,
All night our houses are full of mosquitoes.
The poor people are as thin as a piece of bone,
Because of starvation, diseases often kill them.

Right up until 1949 the ideas of Confucius, a philosopher who lived more than 500 years before the birth of Christ, were still used to keep the people in their place.

Women in China

For more than 2 000 years women in China had to abide by the Three Obediences and Four Virtues laid down by Confucius. The Three Obediences stated that a woman should obey her father and elder brothers when young, her husband when married and her sons when widowed. The Four Virtues demanded that she should know her place, hold her tongue, take care to look attractive and do the housework willingly.

In practice this meant that Chinese women were among the most oppressed in the world. Poverty forced them into marriage at an early age, but they had no choice in whom they would marry. Weddings were arranged for them by their parents and were more like business deals than love-affairs. Child marriages were usual, though young girls were also bought and sold into prostitution as an alternative to marriage. They had no say in the matter. It was quite common for wealthy men to have a number of wives and several mistresses. Their main duty was to produce children and from an early age their feet were bound to restrict their movement and to be a sign of their slave-like existence.

They weren't allowed to divorce their husbands and if their husbands died they couldn't remarry. But husbands could get rid of them any time they liked, leaving them penniless, ridiculed and despised. Old Chinese sayings, like 'noodles are not rice and women are not human beings', and 'a wife married is like a pony bought, I'll ride her and whip her as I like', vividly describe the attitude to women in old China.

They weren't allowed to work in the fields either because it was believed that potatoes planted by a woman wouldn't sprout and melons planted by a woman would be bitter. It was thought improper for them to expose any part of their bodies except their face and hands, and even in an emergency, like a drought or a flood, they weren't allowed to help the men-folk save the crops.

Liberation

The Chinese look back to the period before 1949 as 'the bitter past'. On October of that year came LIBERATION. After a tough war with Japan and a Civil War at home, the People's Republic of China was set up under the leadership of the Communist Party and its Chairman, Mao Tse Tung. Since then things have changed very much and very quickly.

Marriage and Family Life

One of the first things that the new communist government did after liberation was to introduce new marriage laws which did away with the buying and selling of young girls, arranged marriages and prostitution. There was to be no discrimination against illegitimate children, and divorce, though frowned upon, was to be granted at once if both partners wanted it.

By law women couldn't marry until eighteen and men had to wait until twenty-two. But today late marriages are encouraged — twenty-five for women and twenty-eight for men is usual. The Chinese believe that the early twenties are the years in which a young person should study and work hard and that marriage shouldn't be allowed to interfere.

Anna Coote, a reporter, recently visited China to see how things have changed since liberation. Madame Li was typical of the Chinese women she met there.

'Madame Li had married at twenty-four. Her husband was a hospital administrator. The marriage had been a simple affair. No vows, no reception, no honeymoon. Just a quick visit to the local government office to say that they loved each other and had decided to marry. Now they have two children and live in two small rooms with Madame Li's mother, sharing a kitchen and bathroom with four other families.

'She rarely sees her children. The eldest, a three-year-old boy, boards out at a nursery school. Her baby daughter is looked after by the grandmother. She seemed to consider this entirely natural and had no sense of guilt about neglecting her offspring. When we met representatives of the

Like Madame Li most married women earn their own living — working alongside men, as the photograph shows. This has meant changes in family life and schooling, as Anna Coote also discovered.

Women's Federation in Shanghai, we told them that women in the West were often warned that their children might suffer psychological damage if parted too long from their parents at an early age. Were there any signs of this in China? An emphatic 'No'. No evidence of psychological damage at all.

'Madame Li had decided not to have any more children. If contraception let her down, she would have an abortion and be sterilized. She would just go to the hospital and have the operation. No fuss, no waiting, no awkward questions. 'The spread of family planning, nurseries, and public dining, washing and sewing facilities has greatly reduced the burden of domestic work which women previously had to bear. The Communist Party encourages husband and wife to share the remaining domestic chores equally and every married couple we met claimed that they did. 'In the kindergartens and schools we visited, there were few signs that girls and boys were being taught different roles – certainly fewer than one would find in most schools. As far as lessons were concerned, there appeared to be no segregation at any level.

'Girls are trained to think of themselves as workers long before they consider the prospect of marriage and motherhood.'

Anna Coote (Guardian)

YOUR OWN RESEARCH

Make a study of how China has changed since 1949. What problems created by the 'bitter past' had to be overcome and how did the Chinese go about solving them?

Two useful books are:
 China: Inside the People's Republic (Bantam Books 1972)
 Probe 18 : China (SCM Press)

You can also get up-to-date information by writing to:

The Society for Anglo-Chinese Understanding,
152 Camden High Street,
London N W 1.

Try to include detailed information about the following aspects:

China before 1949
The rule of the Emperors, the influence of Confucius, the revolution in 1911 led by Dr Sun Yat-sen, the period of civil war (1925-1949) between the landlords led by Chiang Kai-shek and the communists led by Mao Tse Tung, the war against Japan (1931-1945).

Life of the People before 1949
The peasants, family life, the role of women.

The Thoughts of Chairman Mao
and their influence on China today. What do the Chinese people mean by 'communism', 'walking on two legs', 'serving the people' and 'the cultural revolution'?

Life of People in China Today
People's communes, family life, education, the changed role of women, improvements in the standard of living, health and medicines, leisure activities and entertainments.

1 Explain the meaning of the term nuclear family.
2 What is another name for an extended family?
3 Which religious group celebrates Ramadan?
4 What is meant by the term 'stereotype'?
5 Why are jobs like mechanic, driver and police officer still mainly done by men?
6 What proportion of doctors in 1971 were women in a) Britain and b) Russia?
7 When did the Sex Discrimination Act become law?
8 Name the special Board set up by the government to investigate cases of sex discrimination.
9 What's another word for 'mercy killing'?
10 Why do the Chinese refer to the time before October 1949 as the 'bitter past'?

DOES LOVE NEED MARRIAGE?

Most people in Britain today either want to get married or are married already. But a growing number of people are beginning to ask themselves whether it might be better to live together without getting legally married. Those who think like this are still in a minority; the vast majority of people are horrified by such an idea. But there are signs in other countries, America and Sweden, for example, that an increasing number of young people are choosing not to marry.

They think that marriage is a way of restricting their freedom to come and go as they like. People who love each other shouldn't need a legal contract to keep them together and they should be free to leave when that love dies.

Others believe that marriage is important. If people are joined together by law they will take their duties and responsibilities to each other more seriously. Their relationship will be more secure and a better base from which to bring up children.

But not all marriages provide love and security and a good upbringing for children, and not all the people who live together behave in a thoughtless or irresponsible way.

Perhaps if a relationship is good and children receive love and security it doesn't matter whether people are married or not. But on the whole our society doesn't think like that.

1 a) Make a list of the reasons why you think people get married.

   b) In what ways are young people encouraged to marry by tradition, public opinion, the legal system, the mass media?

   c) What are the advantages and disadvantages of being married from a woman's point of view; from a man's point of view?

2 Make a list of the reasons people might have for chosing to live together without getting legally married. What are the advantages and disadvantages of living together from a woman's point of view; from a man's point of view?

Evelyn Home, the editor of the 'problem page' in *Woman*, received this letter:

'Colin and I got married seven months ago and to be honest it seems like seven years. He wants me to stay on full time at work for at least another two years, but he doesn't stop to think that I get dead tired and could do with a bit of help. We live in a six-roomed house and I do all the cooking, cleaning, washing and ironing while he sits watching me. He wonders why I fall asleep when we go out, but if I ask him to help he says "Just wait until this film ends" or "Hold on while I have a cigarette". I start work at 7.30 a.m. and am still on the go after 11 at night. He goes off to bed when he feels like it and expects me to do the same, but how can I? He leaves his things all over the place and I sometimes think he's only doing it to get me mad.'

Explain fully what advice you would give to the writer of this letter if you were Evelyn Home.

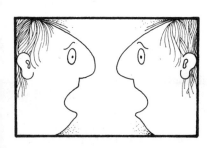

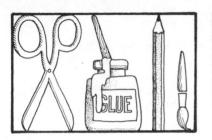

1

Make a collection of Andy Capp cartoons from the *Daily Mirror* over a period of two to three weeks. Though amusing and exaggerated, they are, in some ways, fairly true to life. Describe the main characteristics of the Capps' marriage using examples from the cartoons to illustrate your account.

2

Make a study of divorce in Britain. What proportion of marriages in Britain end in divorce? What are some of the causes of marriage breakdown? What are the legal grounds for divorce? How did the Divorce Reform Act, which came into effect in 1971, change things? How do people go about getting a divorce? What are some of the emotional effects on the couple and children involved?

3

Make a detailed comparison of the prices in local shops and supermarkets and produce a 'guide for consumers' on where to get the best value for money.

4

Some people believe that a group of adults and children who aren't necessarily related can share a home together more happily than a good many families. They believe it's less selfish this way. Children benefit from having lots of adults around and from not being the possessions of their parents. Adults are more independent and can benefit from living with a number of other people. These groups are called COMMUNES. Many grow their own food, rear their own animals and make their own clothes. Make a study of the pros and cons of living in communes compared to living in an ordinary family.

5

In Israel the KIBBUTZIM (singular – KIBBUTZ) have been in operation now for over sixty years. They are communities of people usually living in small farming villages. Everyone has a job to do, work is shared and taken in turns, and in return people receive whatever they need to live on. No one uses any money. Some kibbutzim have their own industries. The ideas behind the kibbutzim and their development over the years have had some interesting effects on the bringing-up of children, education and family life. Some people from Britain go to spend periods of time in Israeli kibbutzim as a means of experiencing a very different way of life.

Find out about the ideas behind the kibbutzim and how they work out in practice.

6

Work out the costs of an average 'white wedding' by finding out the approximate price of the following: the licence, the hire of the church and the choir, the bride's and groom's clothes, the bridesmaids' dresses, the wedding-cake, hire of the cars, a reception for fifty people, photographs, a week's honeymoon in London.

7

This badge is the symbol of the Women's Liberation Movement. Find out all you can about the movement and why they think that women still need to fight for equal opportunities with men.

8

As we've seen, families in China are both similar and dissimilar to those in Britain. Choose any other society you're interested in and make a detailed study of its family life. Give some background information about the society you've chosen. Describe how marriage partners are selected. What are the most common family problems?

Comment on the roles of men, women, children and the elderly. How is the family affected by the world of work?

9

Write a short story or play to illustrate some of the joys and troubles of a young married couple who decide to swap roles completely.

10

Choose any of the jobs shown on p.92-4 to describe in your project. Try to show both the good and the bad aspects of the job.

7 HOUSING

Homing pigeons don't get their name for nothing. Set them free — even miles away from where they live — and they'll find their way back home. Home is even more important to you and me because it's the base from which we go out into the world and live our lives.

Of course people's houses vary. They can tell you a lot about the people who live in them; not just about their taste in decorations or whether they're tidy or not, but also about their social class and how poor or privileged they are in society.

Even today many houses in Britain are not fit places to live in. They should have been pulled down years ago and their occupants given something better. Other people are even worse off; they have no homes at all.

Owning a big expensive house is not in itself the key to happiness. Neither does poor housing mean that the families who live in them are unhappy. But as we shall see, there is a vast difference between the houses of the rich, the not-so-rich and the poor. And this difference has a big influence on their way of life.

RATING THE ENVIRONMENT

One thing which helps to show the difference between good and bad houses is the ENVIRONMENT in which they are built. Environment means all the things which surround where we live.

Some country environments can be beautiful — full of trees, green fields and good fresh air. But in others atomic energy stations, cement works and electricity pylons are just some of the eyesores which spoil the view and POLLUTE the atmosphere.

In towns good environments generally have clean air, spacious tree-lined roads with not too much traffic, buildings in good repair, gardens and open spaces and pavements free of litter. Poor urban environments, like the decaying centres of some of our industrial towns, are dirty and dilapidated, often noisy, frequently smelly and sometimes congested by traffic. There are few trees or parks, but bomb-sites and half-demolished houses make waste-heaps out of open spaces.

People today are very keen to protect the environment from air and noise pollution. Demonstrations are held to 'save the countryside' from destruction by chemicals and poisonous waste. But we mustn't forget that the city environment in which most people live should also be a cause for concern. Good environments have to be protected. Bad ones ought to be changed. How would you rate the environment around your school?

1 Look at the Environment Rating Chart. It shows some of the things which contribute to good and bad environments. Add four more of your own.

2 In each case put a tick in the column which most closely describes the area around your school.

3 Add up the score. The higher the score, the better the environment.

Use the chart to rate other areas of the town. Which areas in your opinion have the best environments and which the worst?

	*****	****	***	**	*
LITTER					
NOISE					
SMOKE, SMELLS & FUMES					
CONDITION OF BUILDINGS & STREET FURNITURE					
TREES & GARDENS					
TRAFFIC CONGESTION					
SCORE	10	8	6	4	2

Key

***** Excellent Environment

**** Good Environment

*** Average Environment

** Unsatisfactory Environment

* Poor Environment

PLANNING A TRAIL

Legend:
1. Hillfield Information Shop
2. New Shopping Precinct
3. Working Mens Club
4. Sheltered Flats
5. De Vere Hostel
6. Lucas Aerospace factory
7. St. Peters Vicarage

⟶ trail route

HILLFIELDS TRAIL

Each day hundreds of people walk the pavements of our villages, towns and cities, scarcely noticing the things they pass by. Perhaps they're aware of the beautiful and the famous sites which visitors come to see, but there are lots of other things worth looking at which are too often taken for granted.

One way of encouraging people to really look at their surroundings is by making a trail. This is a specially planned route around a particular area, which can be walked by anyone who's interested. Usually a detailed map is provided with places of interest marked on. Each trail follower also needs a special guide-book with directions, questions to think about, and notes giving background information on the things to be seen.

Nature trails around country beauty-spots, pointing out different plants and birds are already quite popular. But in towns and cities the things worth looking at aren't always so beautiful.

For those who are interested in 'studying society' town and city trails should consider different kinds of housing and shops, what the environment is like, the history and customs of the area and the way of life of the people who live there. Good trails should encourage the walkers to think about what they see and to decide whether they approve or disapprove of it.

This trail is round part of the Hillfields district of Coventry. Unless you know the area the map won't mean very much to you. But if you also had a set of guide notes and you followed the route shown, you'd see a great variety of interesting, exciting and disturbing things.

. . .the houses in Hood Street and Read Street were built in the 19th century and are now due to be pulled down. Alex's cafe on Hood Street is recommended for chat, friendliness and stuffed cabbage ... . the Chrysler factory on Canterbury Street started life as a Singer sewing machine factory . . . the terrace in Charles Street has been declared buildings of architectural interest by the Department of the Environment . . .

. . . .nearly all the buildings in Primrose Hill Street were pulled down to make way for the Sidney Stringer School. It was once a famous watch-making area. . . .

. . .Southfields school, now a hundred years old, is due to be replaced by new buildings, but like other plans for the area it has been postponed a number of times. . . .

. . .the derelict vicarage at the top of Paynes Lane has an interesting history. It was the base for the Women's Suffrage Movement in Coventry at the beginning of the century and for the Christian Socialist League and the Fabian Society. Residents resent the fact that it lies empty today and want it to be used as a community centre. . . .

In groups of three or four plan a trail of your own. You'll need to produce a map and guide notes, directions and instructions for those who are going to follow it.

Here are some things to consider:

1 Decide first of all whom the trail is for. And then think about the kind of things they'd be particularly interested in. e.g. is it for: tourists who want to see famous sites; people concerned to preserve good environments and to improve bad ones; people interested in architecture, history, art, sketching or photography; foreigners interested to find out about the 'British way of life'; new-comers to the neighbourhood; school pupils making a study of their area.

2 Walk round the route yourselves making detailed notes about what you intend to include. Mark in good vantage points along the route (e.g. slopes, hills, walls) for viewing, sketching or photo-graphing the sites. Make sure the route is neither too long to be tiring nor too short to be over too soon.

3 Mark shelters along the trail if the weather is bad and be careful about road and traffic hazards for walkers who are very young or very old.

4 Encourage the walkers to use all their senses. Besides using their eyes, are there any smells, sounds, tastes or things to touch, worth drawing their attention to?

5 Make sure the guide notes are accurate and well researched. Make sure they're up to date and interesting. Include photographs or sketches of your own as well as written information.

6 Every trail will vary depending on the area, but try to include as many aspects as you can. Here are some suggestions – add as many others of your own as you can:
arcades, archways, architectural styles, banks, baths, bingo-halls, breweries, bridges, cafés, canals, car-parks, chapels, churchyards, cinemas, conservation areas, condition, doorways, factories, farms, flats, fountains, gardens, gasworks, glass, gravestones, hazards, hospitals, houses, history, improvements, ironwork, notices, offices, paths, plaques, play-areas, pubs, pylons, railways, schools, shelter, shops, signs, smells, sounds, safety, size, street-lighting, town hall, view, vacant land, warehouses, woods, works, zoos.

10 When you've produced a map, notes and instruc-tions, invite a group of friends, parents or local residents to try out your trail. Try out one of the trails produced by another group in your class.

11 Arrange a meeting for all those who followed the trail to talk about what they saw, what they learned and what they thought about it. After listening to their comments, suggest ways in which your trail could possibly be improved.

HOUSING CHOICE

Some tenants find themselves in areas which are being redeveloped. Usually they don't have much of a say in what is done. But houses and neighbour-hoods are things which most people have an opin-ion about. Given a choice they know what they would like. One way of finding out is by the 'Housing Choice Game'.

Try the game out for yourselves first, according to the instructions on the opposite page. Then make some copies of the charts. Choose a neigh-bourhood near your school in which the houses are due for redevelopment. Ask about twenty people to make their 'Housing Choice'.

When they've finished, do some arithmetic to see how much money was spent on each choice in each chart by adding all twenty choices together.

The total for chart 1 may look something like this:

CHART 1	£50	£100	£200
House	£200	£800	£1200
Housing Arrangement	£300	£900	£400
Garden		£600	£800
Garage		£500	
Bathroom		£200	£1200
Play facilities	£400		£500
Traffic		£600	£900
Other		£500	

Remember that all together the total amount of money spent on each chart should be 20 people x £500 = £10 000.

1 Which of the preferences on both charts were most popular and had the most money spent on them?
2 Make a list of the three most popular preferences (in order of importance) on each chart.
3 What other important facilities did people include on the bottom line of each chart?

4 Write a report in the form of 'Recommendations to the Council on the Redevelopment of .... Neighbourhood'. Give full details of your findings and make suggestions about how the neighbourhood could best be redeveloped.

Instructions
Your neighbourhood is going to be redeveloped by the council. Imagine that you have a say in how it's to be done.

1 Look at the two charts. One shows the kind of house you could have. The other deals with nearness to places you might want to visit.
2 In this game you have £1000 to spend, £500 on each chart.
3 Look at Chart 1 first of all. Put a cross through each square you would like to buy in order of preference, until you have spent £500. Then do the same for Chart 2.
4 If you think something important has been missed out, please write it in the space provided at the bottom of each chart.

Chart 1 HOUSE AND NEIGHBOURHOOD

	£50	£100	£200
TYPE OF HOUSE	terraced	semi-detached	detached
GARDEN	none	small	large
GARAGE	none	a little way away	by the house
HOUSING ARRANGEMENT	streets	cul-de-sacs	squares
BATHROOM	none	combined	separate
PLAY FACILITIES FOR CHILDREN	none	street closed to traffic	adventure playground
TRAFFIC	no restrictions	no cars allowed	subways under roads
OTHER (please specify)			

Chart 2 TRAVELLING DISTANCES

	£50	£100	£200
WORK	40 mins	20 mins	10 mins
LOCAL SHOPS	20 mins	10 mins	5 mins
FAMILY	20 mins	10 mins	5 mins
FRIENDS	20 mins	10 mins	5 mins
CHURCH	20 mins	10 mins	5 mins
LOCAL PUB	20 mins	10 mins	5 mins
BINGO OR FOOTBALL GROUND	20 mins	10 mins	5 mins
OTHER (please specify)			

PRIVATE HOUSING

People who own the houses they live in are called OWNER OCCUPIERS. The size and value of their houses vary enormously, from old terraced cottages, to large rambling manors.

As a general rule, smaller private houses on new estates are being bought by young married couples and families who need to save very hard to afford even the cheapest houses. People who are wealthier, for example, solicitors, bankers, businessmen and doctors, may well choose larger houses in a suburban road giving them more privacy and space. The very wealthy who can afford to pay the highest prices for their houses will expect lots of space, total privacy and what they believe to be the most beautiful environments.

But whatever the size, owning property is an advantage in our sort of society. So that even though prices have soared in the last few years and people complain bitterly about MORTGAGE repayments, the number of home owners has increased. But what has also increased is the gap between those who can afford to buy houses and those who have no possible hope of ever doing so.

Look at the chart opposite. It shows the advantages of owning, for example, a middle-sized, middle-priced house.

1 Four of the advantages marked £ are to do with money. Explain each of them as fully as you can.
2 Why are choice, space and privacy seen as advantages?
3 Some people have no choice. They have to go where the Council sends them or rent whatever rooms are available. Which of these statements do you most agree with?
   a) 'Everyone should have the same kind of houses, bigger if they have more children, smaller if they don't.'
   b) 'People who have money to spend on houses have a right to buy the best they can. It's just hard luck for the rest.'
   c) 'To own your own house should be a basic human right enjoyed by everybody; it shouldn't be a privilege.'
   d) 'There aren't enough houses to go round for everyone to have a choice. The system is all right as it is.'
   Be able to give reasons for your answer and justify it.
4 Not everyone wants space and privacy. What are the advantages and disadvantages of living in houses close to other houses?

5 What is the job of an estate agent? Who pays him?
6 Working in small groups, make a class survey of housing values in your area.
   a) Look at houses which are advertised for sale in the local newspaper. Choose one and take a photograph of it or draw it.
   b) Describe the environment surrounding the house.
   c) What is the price of the house?
   d) Make a wall display entitled 'The Cost of Private Housing in _____.'
   (Ask an estate agent to help you if necessary and explain politely to the owner what you are doing.)
7 Investigate the business of buying or selling a house. Divide into groups of two or three and ask your teacher to help you contact someone in the area who is buying or selling a house. Make a list of the various stages which the buyer or seller has to go through. Describe any problems which were involved in buying or selling the house.
8 Make a collection of pictures from newspapers and magazines for a scrapbook on housing. Try to show the contrasts between the houses of the wealthy, the not-so-wealthy and the poor.

THE ADVANTAGES OF OWNING A HOUSE

Choice of where to live

Ownership of property which increases its value all the time

Paying for a mortgage means being entitled to certain Income Tax allowances

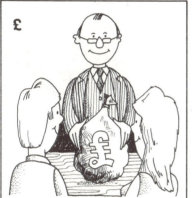

People who own their own houses are able to get credit more easily from banks

Space inside the house — plenty of room for growing children

Space and privacy outside — room for garden and garage

Security for a widow or widower and something to leave as an inheritance

WHAT IS A SLUM?

These pictures were taken by Shelter (the National Campaign for the Homeless) to show houses which are unfit to live in but which are still inhabited because the families who live there have nowhere else to go.

The men and women responsible for deciding whether houses are 'fit for human habitation' are the Environmental Health Officers employed by the council. When they inspect a house they ask themselves several important questions:

1 Is the house safe? Will the roof, floor or walls give way?
2 Does the house need a lot of repairs?
  Can they be done easily and at a reasonable cost?
3 Is there any damp? How bad is it? Can it be cured?
4 Is there enough natural light?
5 How good is the ventilation?
6 Is the water supply adequate?
  Is there hot water?
7 Is there satisfactory drainage, a bathroom and inside lavatory?
8 How easy is it to cook and store food?

If the house doesn't come up to standard then the officer can declare it 'unfit for human habitation'. Usually in poor housing the homes fail on nearly all counts. Yet despite all this, the houses are still occupied — sometimes overcrowded — by families who have no alternative but to live there. The number of houses which could be called slums are not difficult to find. Shelter has seen to that. Part of their attempt to get something done has been to make sure that government and local authorities know just how big the problem is.

SHELTER AND HOMELESSNESS

Make a study of the work of Shelter. They will be happy to send you information to help you with your project if you write to them at Shelter, 86, The Strand, London WC2R 0EQ. A good book from the library is *I Know it was the Place's Fault* by Des Wilson. You may also find a local branch of Shelter in your own town.

Here are some questions to consider:

1 How and why did Shelter start?
2 What methods does it use to fulfil its aims?
3 Who are the homeless?
4 What are the latest figures of homelessness and poor housing nationally and in your area?
5 Why is there a housing problem in Britain?
6 What are the effects of slum housing on people's health and family life and on children's upbringing and education?
7 What is the difference between slum clearance, renewal and redevelopment?
8 Include photographs, a poem, a painting or a model of your own to express what you feel about homelessness.

MULTI-STOREY FLATS

Many conflicting things have been said about living in multi-storey flats as this collection of comments show.

Flats provide opportunities for social and community life.	Flat life is lonely. It's hard to make friends.
Lifts mean there are no problems in living high off the ground.	Lifts are noisy and are always breaking down.
The good view from high flats is a popular feature of flat living.	Living so high up creates feelings of being away from people.
Children in flats are in less danger from traffic.	Balconies, windows and lifts are places of danger to children.
It's easy to keep an eye on children in flats.	Children are always under their mother's feet.
Mothers enjoy their new, modern homes.	Lonely mothers, confined in their flats, often become depressed and neurotic.

Which view is right? The people most likely to know are the people who live in multi-storey flats. But before asking them, look at the research findings in more detail.

NO CYCLING
NO BALL GAMES

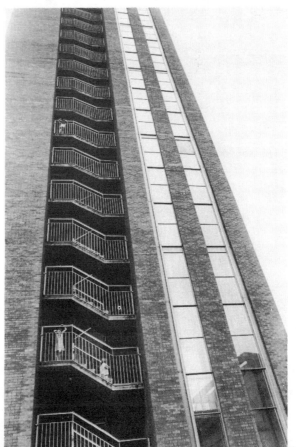

MULTI-STOREY FLATS – RESEARCH FINDINGS

These are some of the things which research studies have found out about living in multi-storey flats.

Health

Families living in flats are more likely to be ill and to visit the doctors than house dwellers. Illness is caused by being cramped in a small space. Women may become depressed and neurotic.
(*Families in Flats*, D. Fanning)

Space

Many flats are badly designed and provide little usable space. Hall space is either in short narrow corridors which give the feeling of being cramped, or wide hallways taking up room which might have been used for living accomodation. Bedrooms tend to be for sleeping in only and are therefore small.

Children confined in a small space have little or no room for their own activities. They are also likely to get under their mother's feet. This may well make mothers short-tempered with their children.
(*Children in Flats*, NSPCC)

Noise

Lifts, stairways, machinery and pumping apparatus in flats all make noises which irritate flat dwellers.
(*Problem of Flat Life*, J. Macey)

Coming and going

There are three main ways of getting into flats as these drawings show.

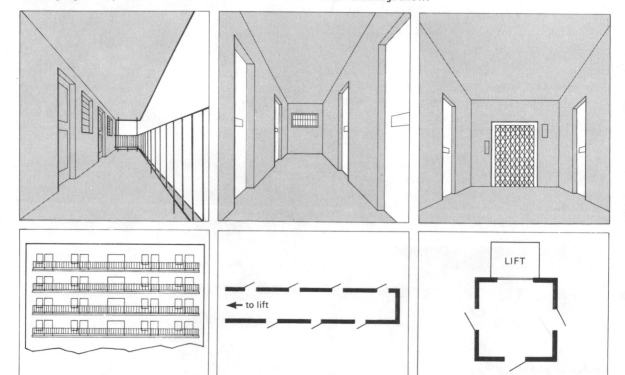

Gallery (balcony) access   Corridor access   Landing (well) access

Each type has its own advantages and disadvantages. Lots of people in flats complain about the lifts. Apart from the noise, they often break down. People living on high storeys don't go out as much as those living on lower floors because of the inconvenience of the lifts.
(*Living Off the Ground*, Reynolds and Nicholson)

Loneliness

People in flats, especially women, complain again and again about loneliness. Corridors full of unfriendly closed doors, windows which look down on a world of midgets, the local shop at least twenty storeys away, all add to the problem.

Children miss important contacts with other children. Isolated and without proper play facilities they become either shy or over-boisterous.
(*Children in Flats*, NSPCC)

Play facilities

In multi-storey flats childrens play areas are often out of sight of their parents. Playgrounds are often tatty. A few swings, a slide, a climbing frame and a dirty or unfilled sandpit are about the best that is provided. Signs saying 'KEEP OFF THE GRASS' are still common. Very few flats provide inside play facilities.
(*Children in Flats*, NSPCC)

1　Look at the pictures on page 113. Even without words they have a lot to say about multi-storey flats. What do the pictures tell you about life in multi-storey flats? Make a photographic study of your own about multi-storey flats. Try to take photographs which show exactly what you think and feel about them. Include picture studies of the buildings, the environment round about and the people who live in the flats. Take some photographs inside too. Your teacher will advise you about cameras, films and flashes if you need help. Present your study either in a scrap-book or as a wall display.

2　Look at the drawings on page 114. Make a list of the advantages and disadvantages of each of these entry arrangements.

3　Explain what the NSPCC study of *Children in Flats* said about space, loneliness and play facilities. What were two of the problems of flat life reported by J. Macey and D. Fanning?

4　Write to the Director of Housing in your area and find out
　　a) how many people are housed in multi-storey flats.
　　b) if the council intends to build any more multi-storey flats.
　　c) if the council has any views about housing old people in multi-storey flats.
　　d) if the council has any views about housing families with young children above the fifth storey.
　　e) what play facilities are provided inside and outside council flats.

5　Arrange to interview some residents of multi-storey flats and find out what they think about living there, what other types of houses they've lived in and how these compare with the flats. Discuss the comments and research findings on pages 114 and 115. Include questions in your interview which will give you information about health, space, noise, comings and goings, loneliness and play facilities in flats. Write a report to compare your findings with those of the experts.

6　Some people love their flats (despite what the experts say!). Others hate them. Make a tape-recording of two residents who have opposite opinions. Get them to say in detail what they like or dislike. Have one or two questions ready about noise, loneliness and facilities, for example, in case they begin to 'dry-up'.

ARE THERE GYPSIES AT THE BOTTOM OF YOUR GARDEN ?

'Gypsies at the bottom of your garden . . . We are sorry for any disturbance we have caused you. Why are we camping here? We have been forced out of the traditional sites where our families have camped for centuries. Some of us have bought our own bit of land, but we cannot even camp there because we've been refused planning permission. Under the 1968 Caravan Sites Act, Lambeth Borough Council has a legal obligation to provide our families with a site, where we could park our caravans and pay weekly rent. We want our children to go to school, but what chance of education do they have while we're being pushed on from place to place? We hope you will give us your support — all we ask is somewhere to live; if we're moved on from here, WHERE DO WE GO?'

This letter was circulated by gypsies illegally parked in Geneva Road, Lambeth, to local residents. Lambeth has hundreds of homeless families. It also has thirty traveller families. Another London borough, Ealing, has hundreds of immigrant families in badly overcrowded conditions. It also has forty traveller families, camped illegally and in constant fear of eviction.

The gypsies or travellers may sound like a minority but there are about 5 000 such families in Britain and they nearly all suffer from the prejudice and hostility of our society.

Three-quarters of these families have no legal place to live. They don't have to share washing and toilet facilities with five other families — they have

no washing facilities. Their children don't go to old, run-down city schools — they mostly don't go to *any* school. It's not easy to send your child off to school in the morning when the police may well have moved you on by the afternoon.

The gypsies' traditional crime has been their refusal to conform. A hundred years ago you could be sent to the gallows just for associating with gypsies. Today gypsies aren't hanged but they are threatened with violence, turned off their land and moved on from one roadside, quarry or rubbish dump to another.

In 1968 the Caravan Sites Act was passed and came into effect in 1970. The Act said that it was the duty of every local authority to provide a site for gypsies in their area. They had to provide at least fifteen places for caravans but once this had been done they could throw out and impose heavy fines on any other gypsies who tried to camp there. Since 1970 only a small number have been built and three-quarters of the gypsy population still have nowhere legal to stay.

This raises several important issues:

1 Why have some local authorities not yet provided camp sites for gypsies?
2 Why do some local authorities only provide the minimum number of places when they have more than fifteen gypsy families in their area?
3 Can gypsies who find places on permanent sites still continue their traditional way of life, e.g. moving about the country to find seasonal employment, keeping animals, collecting and sorting scrap metal, cooking on open fires and eating out of doors?
4 Do local authorities provide extra facilities for friends and relatives who come to visit the gypsy sites? Family ties are strong among gypsies and ceremonies like births, marriages and anniversaries are times for great celebrations.
5 Are there any transit-sites or places where gypsies can legally stay for a few nights or weeks before moving off somewhere else?
6 Do local authorities provide any special schools for the gypsies or are they trying to get gypsy children to attend ordinary schools?
7 What is the attitude of local residents to the gypsies? Are their opinions about gypsies based on fact, fear or prejudice?

Find out the answers to these questions by discussing them together and then by writing to the local authority, the Gypsy Council and the Romany Guild. Before contacting the local authority make sure you know something about the gypsy way of life. Here are some suggestions to help you:

1 Make detailed notes on gypsy history, customs and traditions.
2 How do gypsies in Britain today earn their living?
3 What fears and prejudices do people have about gypsies? What problems do gypsies trying to preserve their traditional way of life experience in Britain today?
  Give examples of cases where gypsies have been treated badly by local residents, the police and local authorities.

4 Are there any gypsy families in your area?
  Has a decent site been provided for them?
  Could the local authority do more to help them?
  How do the local residents treat them?
  Do the gypsies cause any problems in the area?

Some useful books

Men of the Road, Charles King
The Book of Boswell, Silvester Gordon Boswell
Gypsies and Other Travellers, HMSO
On the Road, Grattan Puxon

Useful Addresses

The Gypsy Council
343, Garrat Lane,
London SW18.

The Romany Guild
c/o Tom Lee,
The Caravan Site,
Folly Lane,
Walthamstow,
London E17.

DOWN AND OUT

Charlie may stay most nights at the Strand Palace Hotel, be seen often at Covent Garden, and lunch most days at the Temple, but he's not a snob. They are, he explains, simply the best places, and that's not saying much, because the alternatives for Charlie are Waterloo Station, derelict buildings, park benches or the dosshouse.

Charlie is a dosser. So he never enters the Strand Palace by the front door – in fact, he's never been inside the place. He stays in the alley at the back, one of a huddle of men who keep themselves alive in winter with the warmth from the air vent linked to the hotel's central heating. As for Covent Garden, he goes there for the nightly performance of the 'soup run'. That and the free tea and bread obtainable in the Temple at lunch time stand between him and starvation.

There are thousands more like him: the authorities put the figure at around 30 000; voluntary organizations reckon it exceeds 40 000 and is increasing.

Their homelessness is the common factor. Otherwise they may look alike, but their basic problems are very different. Up to a third are likely to be mentally ill. Almost another third range from men with drinking problems to chronic alcoholics. The remainder reflect unemployment or bad luck. Nearly all of them are in poor health, and many of them are clearly ill.

It is a fairly simple matter for the authorities to pass more compassionate legislation and to advocate more humane policies. It's not so simple for local authorities to find the money to carry them out.

There seems to be a need for four different types of accommodation: for after-care of patients discharged from mental hospitals; for ex-prisoners; for alcoholics and drunken offenders; and for the dosser who, for whatever reason, will always be a dosser and asks only for a place to sleep and cheap meals.

The failure of local authorities to provide for former mental patients makes the problem worse. The aim of the 1959 Mental Health Act was to move people out of hospitals into the community, but because of poor provision, there are today as many as 30 000 people virtually 'imprisoned' in mental hospitals because there is nowhere else for them to go.

Ex-prisoners face a similar problem. Of 40 000 people in prison, over 5000 will have nowhere to go when their time comes to be released. This could well make them return to crime.

As for drunken offenders, a recent Home Office working party recommended special centres for the treatment of alcoholics and drunkards instead of prison or fines. But it said facilities would be required for 2000 men and 2000 women before such a policy would be effective. On present performance one cannot see how such a target could ever be reached.

The musical-comedy picture of the tramp as a fat, jolly beer-drinking character is out of date — if it was ever true. The pitiful heaps of newspapers and old clothing that lie in the darkest corners of our towns and cities are human beings slowly dying of illness and neglect. In many cases no treatment can turn them from the way of life they've adopted, but their simple plea is: 'Even when we're in the gutter we're still human — treat us as human.'

(Adapted from *Minority Report* by Des Wilson)

Find out whether your local authority does anything to help the down and outs. Some areas will have more down and outs than others. Some authorities won't like to admit that they have such problems. But mental illness, crime and drunkenness can effect anyone, whatever social background or area they come from. So often, as Des Wilson explains, these people are neglected and rejected by the rest of society.

1 Contact the Health and Social Services Department and the Police.
   a) Are there any people sleeping rough in the area? Who are they, and where do they sleep?
   b) Are there any hostels for the homeless?
   c) What provision is made for ex-prisoners, after-care patients from mental hospitals, alcoholics and drug addicts in the area?
   d) What is done for youngsters discharged from community homes (approved schools) and borstals?
2 Contact the voluntary organizations in your area which try to help people in trouble.
   a) What kinds of problems do they deal with?
   b) Is enough being done to help?

Here are some groups to contact. Your teacher will advise you about others:

The Samaritans, Child Poverty Action Group, Alcoholics Anonymous, National Association for Mental Health, Shelter, Youth Action, NACRO (National Association for the Resettlement of Offenders), The Salvation Army.

3 Case-study
   a) Choose any one of the down-and-out groups mentioned above and describe clearly
      (i) the nature of their problem.
      (ii) what is being done to help them.
      (iii) where the local authorities and voluntary organizations are failing to help.
   b) Make some recommendations of your own about what should be done.
   c) Try to make your case-study as full of impact as possible by the use of photographs, quotations and descriptive writing.

1 What is meant by the term 'owner occupier'?
2 What is the job of an estate agent?
3 What is a mortgage?
4 Give three examples of different types of pollution.
5 What are the aims of the organization Shelter?
6 Who decides whether a house is fit for human habitation?
7 Which local government department is responsible for housing?
8 Roughly how many gypsy families are there in Britain today?
9 When did the Caravan Sites Act come into effect and what was it designed to do?
10 What was the aim of the 1959 Mental Health Act and why haven't these aims been carried out?

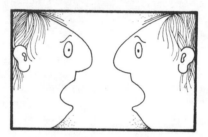

1 What are the problems and queries about housing in your area? They may be to do with slum-clearance, rents, rates or the Council's housing policy. What do your parents and neighbours get angry or confused about? A short survey of the views of local residents will give you some idea of public complaints.

  When you have pin-pointed some of the problems and worked out a few questions, invite local residents and a representative from the local housing department to explain the Council's housing policy and to answer your questions.

2 a) Imagine you are the spokesman of a local residents' group formed to oppose the building of a motorway. It's feared that some houses will have to be pulled down and others will find their gardens backing directly onto the new road. Make a speech outlining your objections in a way which will encourage public support for your views.

  b) Imagine you are the planning officer responsible for the motorway scheme. Make a speech to justify the plan in a way which will encourage people to accept it.

3 Choose an old area of town which everyone agrees ought to be either pulled down or redeveloped. Argue the pros and cons of a) moving the residents out to new estates in the suburbs, b) modernizing and improving the area as it stands or c) pulling down the houses and replacing them with multi-storey flats.

1 GETTING RID OF EYESORES

Many areas have their eyesores — things which spoil the environment. Somewhere near you there might be a clogged-up and dirty canal, waste-ground or a bomb-site where rubbish is tipped, old half-destroyed houses just left to rot. Everybody complains about them, but nobody does anything. Perhaps you could.

Find out who the eyesore belongs to. Are there any plans for its future? Can you help to clean it up or redevelop it?

It's possible, for example, to turn waste land into gardens, bomb-sites into adventure playgrounds, clogged-up canals into pleasant boating and leisure areas. It takes a lot of hard work, time and money. Could you raise some money, give up a little of your spare time and do some hard work to get rid of the eyesore?

2 SOCIAL STUDIES IN PRACTICE

a) Residents in a northern town were worried about the poor conditions of some of their houses. Talking to neighbours, they found they had common problems of damp, decay and subsidence. So they planned to collect information about the extent of the problems in the hope that the Council would declare their neighbourhood a General Improvement Area. This meant a detailed survey of all the houses.

Pupils from the local school had some experience of doing surveys and decided to help.

b) In Bristol pupils identified a traffic problem in one of the roads near their school. No garages and double parking made a busy road even more hazardous. Yet there was a grass verge which provided much wasted space. They collected evidence from householders (who already had good-sized gardens) to show that they would prefer a parking area to the verge. The report was given to the Council who later agreed to carry out its recommendations.

Two examples of ways in which school pupils provided the information which residents needed to get the local Council to take action. Do any 'local campaigns' need similar help in your area?
Or, like the Bristol pupils, can you identify a problem, which causes irritation, but which could be solved by local authority action?
See whether you can put your social studies to some practical use!

1

Make a study of town planning over the last hundred years. When did people begin to take the idea of planning seriously? Include information about garden cities and new towns.

2

Trace the history of old houses in your area. When were they built? Who were they built for? How have their fortunes changed over the years?

3

Design a house specially for an elderly or a handicapped person. What special features would you include? How would you furnish it? Use plans drawn to scale, pictures and models to illustrate your design.

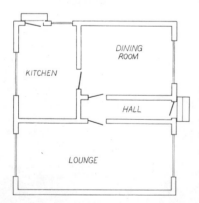

4

Produce a study in words and pictures of a stately home.

5

Make a survey of the houses and their inhabitants in a street near your school. What type of houses are they? Do they have basic amenities, garden and garage, etc? How many inhabitants per house? What proportion of children under five, school children, single people, pensioners live in them? Use bar charts to illustrate your findings.

6

Produce a scrap-book to illustrate and describe homes in other countries. How do they compare with those in Britain?

7

What is meant by the term 'pollution'? Make a list of as many different types of pollution as you can. Describe and illustrate some of their effects on towns and the countryside.

8

What are conservation groups? Describe some of the activities of conservation groups determined to get rid of all types of pollution.

8 COMMUNITY CONCERNS

WHAT MAKES A COMMUNITY ?

'Down this street we're a community. We all know each other like family and help out when it's needed. That's what it's all about. We've got things in common. Most of us grew up around here. Our kids play together and go to the same schools. We work in the same factories and see each other at the Bull's Head two or three nights a week for a drink. You can't beat the community spirit round these parts! Now if we could get the whole country to feel the same about it. And then the world. You wouldn't have to worry about wars and things like that.' (Fred Allen, resident in the same street for forty-three years)

Think about the term 'community'. It's one we use a lot. What does it mean? What exactly is a community? And how does it differ from any ordinary street or village or area where people live? In simple terms, communities have two main characteristics — one to do with space and one to do with people.

A community is an area marked by some kind of boundary-line which locals recognize. The boundary might be a railway-line, a river or a canal, a major road or a large open space. The area often has its own special name like Tiger Bay in Cardiff, Chelsea in London, Clifton in Bristol or the Gorbals in Glasgow. In rural areas a group of farms or a small village might be called a community.

When the people who live there recognize that they've got a lot of things in common; when they share the same schools, shops, pubs, clubs and workplaces; when they see a lot of each other and know all about each other; when these links are often passed on from one generation to the next; then we call the area a community.

When people of the same religion or race live close to others who are the same, they usually do so because they have a lot in common. If they're in a minority in the country as a whole, they probably feel the need for living close to people with the same attitudes and way of life. Often, as they get established, special shops, religious meeting places and clubs are set up and a community life begins.

UPPER-CLASS COMMUNITIES

Upper-class communities are to be found deep in suburban areas like the stock-broker belt of Surrey or the fashionable centres of large towns like Chelsea, Hampstead and Mayfair. The cost of housing is well beyond the reach of most people and this helps to keep the areas privileged and exclusive.

People in upper-class communities obviously have a lot in common too. Wealth, power, influential jobs, expensive home comforts and costly leisure activities are just some of the interests they have a stake in preserving.

MIDDLE-CLASS COMMUNITIES

Middle-class communities tend to be in villages or in the suburbs. There are no factories and the neighbourhood is clean, spacious and pleasantly near to the country-side. The houses are either on small private estates or suburban roads. They are self-contained, owner-occupied and separated from neighbours by carefully tended gardens. The atmosphere is private and peaceful and the residents like it that way.

They don't get too involved in each others' affairs. They may only stay for a few years and then move on to a bigger house or to a better job in another city. Not too involved, that is, unless something threatens their peace and quiet. Middle-class communities suddenly spring into action if the government decides to build a motorway nearby, or to open a mental hospital or prison. They don't like airports, juggernaut lorries, or council estates either.

AFFLUENT WORKERS

Not all working-class communities are characterized by poverty as they once were. Improvements in wages and working conditions over the last twenty years or so have made some working-class people quite well off. This means that they can afford to buy houses on private estates where they may well find themselves living near to teachers, clerical workers and others, usually described as middle-class.

It's doubtful whether neighbourhoods like these can really be called 'communities' though. People live next door to others doing very different kinds of jobs, and their place of work is usually some distance away from where they live. They seem to lack the 'things in common' which are typical of one-class communities, especially traditional working-class communities.

125

TRADITIONAL WORKING-CLASS COMMUNITIES

In old working-class communities, in the industrial centres of large towns the locals and their families have probably lived there for generations. Often the men and women work in the same local industries, use the same corner shops and pubs in the evening. Their children go to the same schools, work in the same industries, and marry boys and girls from neighbouring streets.

Parents speak to the rent man to get nearby houses for their married daughters to live in and they in turn begin to set up families. Old and dilapidated housing, low incomes and unemployment are common experiences of the community. Social Security men and 'the Welfare' are frequent visitors to the streets.

There are areas like 'Coronation Street' where everyone knows everyone else's business. Where families and neighbours depend on each other for help in times of emergency, support in times of trouble and friendship in day-to-day activities.

When the work done by the local people is dangerous, even stronger ties are formed. No mining community or trawler-fishing community lacks its tragedies: men killed or maimed down the pit; trawlers full of husbands, brothers and sweethearts lost beneath sixty-foot waves out at sea. Shared tragedy brings families and neighbours together. Depending on team mates for your own safety at work and being responsible for theirs, makes for close friendships — friendships which don't stop at the dock or the pit gates.

But life isn't all good-heartedness and brotherly love. Bad conditions cause tensions. These are also communities which, in many towns, are in the process of being cleared or redeveloped. Some of the residents are moved out whether they like it or not. Others move to better areas of their own accord. Their places are taken by immigrants who frequently have nowhere else to go.

MULTI-RACIAL COMMUNITIES

In the 1950s Britain couldn't provide enough workers for manual jobs especially in the textile and hosiery business and in public transport. So recruitment offices were set up in the West Indies encouraging workers to emigrate to England. Later they were joined by workers from India and Pakistan. Brought up under British rule in the days of the Empire and later the Commonwealth, they had come to regard themselves as British and to think of England as the 'mother country'. But when they arrived things were very different.

Finding somewhere to live was the first problem. They couldn't qualify for council houses and rents paid to private landlords were often fixed at 'swindle level'. They were therefore forced to accept the old and decaying centres of the industrial towns where they had gone for work.

The houses they had to live in were thrown together around factories built in the nineteenth century. In those days town planning for the poor was not known. The main aim was to cramp the workers as near to each other and to their work-place as possible.

This very close, on-top-of-each-other existence now causes tensions in a multi-racial community. Late night parties, family arguments and the smells of cooking are all shared with neighbours, whether they like it or not.

Older residents blame the newcomers for 'bringing the area down'. Too often immigrants are accused of creating slums. But this isn't fair. The houses were no doubt in a deplorable state before they arrived.

NEW ESTATES AND NEW TOWNS

Those who move out of run-down city communities often go to brand new council estates on the fringes of the town, or to new towns several miles away. The people have something in common — new houses and the same area to live in. But the old social ties have been left behind where they came from and new ones have to be created.

Newcomers often experience isolation and loneliness because they don't know anyone. Multi-storey flats don't have doorsteps to chat on. The corner shop is now a large impersonal supermarket.

Meeting places like pubs, clubs and recreation centres are often the last things to be built.

But once the estates have settled down and the people have settled in then the community feelings begin to develop. Some local authorities try to help this along by moving residents next to people they know. Others plan their estates in ways meant to encourage neighbourly contacts, with little squares, cul-de-sacs and even back-to-back housing arrangements.

RURAL COMMUNITIES

Life in the country sounds very attractive to many town dwellers who are tired of traffic, noise and overcrowding. Where villages are close to towns they can be 'taken over' by house-buyers escaping from the city. In the process, a lot of their community characteristics change.

But in more isolated rural areas village life still continues in the traditional way. Villagers have often lived all their lives in the country, frequently within a few miles of where they were born. Almost all the work in the village comes from farming, but there are also local shop-keepers, a policeman, a vicar and perhaps a school teacher. Nowadays though, villagers increasingly work in industries recently established in rural areas.

Secrets are hard to keep in villages. Everyone knows everyone else's business and milkmen,

postmen and shop-keepers help to spread the gossip around. It's much harder to get away with doing things the community disapproves of in a village than it would be in a large, anonymous town.

Family ties are usually strong and often involve different members of the family working together.

Each village has its traditional 'gentry' of wealthy farmers and its majority of ordinary workers. But old ties of family, employment and neighbourliness often cut across the usual barriers of class and status.

Strangers to the village sometimes find it hard to fit in. People who have lived there for ten or fifteen years are still regarded as newcomers compared to the families who have lived there for generations.

ASKING THE PEOPLE

A lot has been written about the friendliness and community spirit of village life and of working-class neighbourhoods in our big cities. The comment on page 124 explains the views of one man in a traditional working-class street. He and his neighbours don't want to move to a smarter neighbourhood or to a new town. Are his feelings typical? Do people really get attached to old places? Does neighbourliness and familarity make up for bad conditions? Or do people feel trapped in poor areas? Perhaps they lack the money or the opportunity to leave. Maybe they feel there's nothing they can do about changing things. Choose a working-class area like this near you, or a country village, and try to find out what the people who live there feel about their community.

Here are some of the things you should try to find out:

1 Survey
How long have people lived in the area and do their family and relations live nearby?
2 Neighbours
What do people think of their neighbours?
Do they like them and get on with them?
Do they have much to do with them?
Have newcomers arrived in the area? How are they regarded?
3 Friends
Do people's close friends live in the area?
Where do they meet them? How often do they see them?
4 Leisure
Are there places to spend leisure time in the community? What are their favourite leisure activities?
5 HELP
Who would they turn to in times of trouble — close family, relatives, neighbours, friends, social worker, policeman, school teacher, vicar, no one?
6 Likes
What do they think is best about their community?

7 Dislikes
Have they any complaints? What is bad about the area?
8 Action
Have they ever tried to do anything about their complaints?
If yes, how? and with what results?
If no, why not?
9 Moving
If they were to move what would they most miss about the area?
If they didn't live there, where would they like to live?
10 Different Views
In what ways, if any, do the views about the community of young, middle-aged and old people differ?

Questions

Work out some questions first and then interview as many people as you can. Make the questions as short, simple and straightforward as possible. For example, in trying to find out how long people have lived in the area and whether their family and relatives live nearby, you could ask:

How long have you been living here?
Where did you live before?
Why did you leave?
Is this a better place?
Do any other members of your family live in this area?
Do any of your relatives live in this area?

Reporting Back

When you've collected all the information together, write a report on your findings including
1 a description of the area you studied.
2 how you carried out the investigation.
3 an account of what you found out.
4 your views and comments on your findings.

PLANNING AHEAD

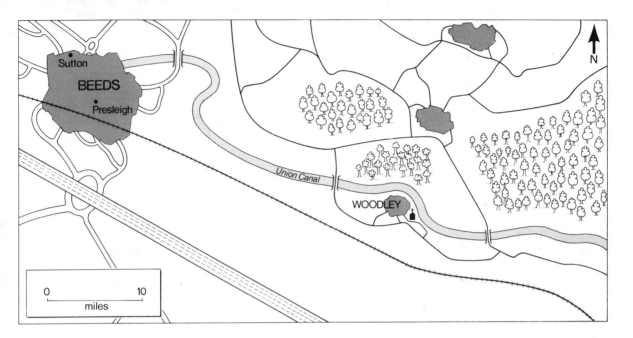

As we saw in Chapter 2, the census gives some of the information governments need to make plans for the future.

Divide into groups of four and imagine that you are a team of town-planners. Your project is to expand a small village called Woodley, with a population of about 800 people, into a new town. The new town will draw most of its population from 'Beeds', a large industrial city about thirty miles away. But it's also hoped to attract settlers from farther afield. The aim is to establish a thriving community with a population of about 80 000 by the year 2001.

You are given statistical information from the most recent census and some facts about the needs of the area. Discuss all the details carefully, make sure you understand them and do any research you need to find out how real planners work.*

Draw up detailed plans and a full report about how you would expand the new town and what facilities you would need to provide. When you're satisfied that you've thought of everything, present your scheme

*Arrange with your teacher for a representative from the local Planning Office or a lecturer in Town Planning to come an explain how real planners would tackle this exercise.

You can also get information about planning from the Department of the Environment (see p. 160).

to the rest of the class for their approval. You can include maps, diagrams and other visual material to illustrate your ideas.

Here is the information the planners are given.

SLUM CLEARANCE

'Presleigh', an area of slum-dwellings and poor environment in Beeds, will be cleared between 1978 and 1986 and the inhabitants encouraged to move to Woodley. It is to be expected that young married couples with small children will be the first to set up home in Woodley.

A MIXED COMMUNITY

It is hoped to encourage a mixed community in Woodley in terms of social class and occupation. The managers and professional workers involved in new industries and services in Woodley will be encouraged to live locally. Commuters to salaried occupations in Beeds will also be encouraged to make Woodley their home.

Woodley is likely to be mixed in terms of races too. Census returns show that a third of the inhabitants of Presleigh are of West Indian origin. It is local authority policy to re-house Asian immigrants living in Sutton, a district to the north of Beeds, in housing of a decent standard – possibly in Woodley.

POPULATION

It is estimated that the number of people living in Woodley will be

15 000 by 1981
35 000 by 1985
50 000 by 1991
80 000 by 2001

The percentage of children under sixteen in the population is expected to be

30% in 1981
50% in 1985
40% in 1991
30% in 2001

The percentage of elderly people in the population is expected to be

2% in 1981
4% in 1985
7% in 1991
10% in 2001

EMPLOYMENT

New industries providing jobs for 30 000 men and women by 2001 must be attracted to the area.

HOUSING

Private and Local Authority (i.e. Council) housing must be available for 80 000 people by 2001.

COMMUNICATIONS

Industrial development and commuting to Beeds will mean that improved road and rail links with the main motorways and centres of trade and business are necessary.

SHOPPING AND LEISURE FACILITIES

These should be a priority to encourage community feeling and involvement and to serve the needs of an expanding population. The high proportion of young married couples and children should be borne in mind here.

PRESENT RESOURCES

Woodley has at present one doctor, one mid-wife, and a part-time social worker to serve its population of 800. There are three shops including a post-office, two churches and two pubs.

The nearest bank is five miles away and a travelling library-van visits the village once a fortnight. The village primary school has two classes and the nearest secondary school is ten miles away. There are no special provisions for the sick, the elderly, the handicapped or those with social problems.

BECAUSE THEY'RE BLACK...

Chris Mullard was born in Hampshire in 1944. He is an Englishman. But he is also black. In his book *Black Britain* he describes how as a child he was taught to be ashamed of his colour. As he grew older he realized that many white opinions about black people are not only cruel but also wildly inaccurate.

He now works as a Community Relations Officer trying to encourage understanding in multi-racial communities, but more especially, self-confidence and pride among black people.

Discuss together these two extracts from his book. The first describes his childhood experiences, the second his feelings now. (As you read them make sure you understand the difficult words written in italics.)

1   In an extremely *subtle* way school taught me to consider the colour of my skin as ugly. My teachers never mentioned my colour. Instead they mentioned the customs of black people in far-off lands, Britain's former role in civilising the natives, making them acceptable to the white man and in turn to themselves. They made me learn *nationalist* songs, recite poetry *enraptured* with the glories of the Empire; they taught me British *etiquette,* how to be nice to everybody and how to *doff* my hat to my superiors. All in all I was a little white boy in black skin. But I took a back row seat whenever *dignitaries* visited the school because I was not white and I was told numerous stories about wicked black people who were responsible for all the troubles in the world. As a teenager I emerged believing that black was wrong, white was right. Whenever asked about my colour, I explained that it was only *superficial.* It was no more than a heavy sun tan which I got from frequent holidays in the Caribbean. *Naively* I stated that beneath the tan I was as white as the next man.
In later years, many miles away from home and school, I associated with *bigots.* I played the part which I thought would bring acceptance. I allowed my leg to be pulled and people to think of me as 'good for a giggle'. Furthermore I did not object to people telling *racial* jokes at my expense. I fast became *subservient* in the hope that people I met would go on treating me as white.

2   At long last we are beginning to reject the white *myths* about ourselves. — we are not lazy; we do not live off the dole; we do not breed like rabbits; we are not the cause of the country's social and political problems; we do not smell; we do not bring down house values; we are not *maladjusted;* we are not *educationally sub-normal;* and emphatically we are not inferior or ugly. Our habits, customs and *cultures* are just as civilised as anybody else's. We are beautiful. We are just as intelligent as others. We are industrious. We possess a sense of *morality.* The work we do is of vital importance to white society. We are proud.

    (from *Black Britain,* by Chris Mullard)

1   From your own knowledge or experience, make a list of the ways in which black people are made to feel 'ugly' and 'inferior' in our society. Think very carefully about the ways black people are portrayed in films, comics, jokes, on television and in news-papers. In what ways is 'black' frequently associated with 'evil', and 'white' with 'goodness'?

2   What is meant by the term 'scapegoat'? How are coloured immigrants used as scapegoats in our society?

3   What is meant by the term 'stereotype'? What is the stereotyped view of Jews, Pakistanis, Americans, Englishmen, Irishmen, Welshmen, Scotsmen, Russians, and Frenchmen? Are stereotypes accurate descriptions of people?

4   What is the difference between 'prejudice' and 'discrimination'? Are there any ways in which coloured people are discriminated against in our society? Is anything done to prevent racial discrimination? What is the Race Relations Board? What is the job of Community Relations Officers?

5   What are racialist jokes? Do you think they serve any useful purpose? Do they increase racial prejudice or help overcome it?

6   How many coloured immigrants are there in Britain? Where do they come from? Why were they encouraged to come here? Why did they want to come?

7   What are the main problems which face black people in multi-racial communities? Do white immigrants experience the same problems?

For more information, contact:

Community Relations Commission,
15-16 Bedford Street,
LONDON WC2E 9HX

Joint Council for the Welfare of Immigrants,
Toynbee Hall,
Commercial Street,
LONDON E1

Race Relations Board,
5, Lower Belgrave Street,
LONDON SW1

UK Immigrants Advisory Service,
St George's Churchyard,
Bloomsbury Way,
LONDON WC1

COMMUNITY RIGHTS AND WRONGS

Accounts like these could be found in most local newspapers. . . .

Squatters Move in to Gladstone Street

Four families moved into the empty houses in Gladstone Street yesterday. They soon put up signs saying 'THIS HOUSE IS OCCUPIED' and 'COUNDON FAMILY SQUATTING ASSOCIATION'.

Jim Henderson, unemployed fitter and father of four children acted as the spokesman for one of the families. 'We have nowhere to live,' he said. 'We've been split up for the last two years and this is the only way we can get together again.' Annie Roberts, a twenty-three-year-old mother of two said, I've been in a hostel for the homeless for the last eighteen months and my husband had to lodge with his brother. Having nowhere to live was breaking up our family.'

Gladstone Street was closed for redevelopment two weeks ago but the Council says the houses might be left empty for months before new building begins. Councillor Surridge said he did not approve of squatting but he was well aware of the problems facing homeless families. He would do all he could to find these people somewhere permanent to live.

I asked Jim Henderson if other families would be joining them. 'They certainly will,' he said. 'These houses aren't in very good nick but at least we can show the Council that they can't forget about us. They'll have to find us somewhere else or carry us out'.

Rick Davis, the local Shelter organiser, was soon on the scene. 'Squatting has become a very effective form of protest.' he said. 'Many local authorities in London now let their empty houses he used by squatters until the redevelopment plans come through.'

He explained that the Family Squatting Advice Service was set up in London in 1970 to help squatters' groups. 'It provides an information sheet about how to start groups and gives advice on legal matters like rates and compulsory purchase.' In time the families move as council houses become available or into privately rented accommodation.

Local Head Sits Down in Street

Children from Norfolk Street Primary School did not go to school yesterday. They sat down in the road with their mothers. The mothers, calling themselves Norfolk Street Action Group or NAG for short, are complaining about the traffic in Norfolk Street.

'My kid has to cross that street four times a day,' said Mrs Beaumont. 'There's no proper crossing and no warden and since that road haulage business moved into the street, the traffic's been terrible.'

Mr Anderson, Head of Norfolk Street Primary School, joined the mothers in their protest. 'I suppose it seems strange to see a Headmaster sitting down in the road,' he said, 'but this might make the Council take action quicker. One six-year-old girl was nearly killed here last week and I want something done soon before anyone gets really hurt.'

About twenty women and thirty-five children joined the protest. They carried a variety of banners with slogans like 'NAG THE COUNCIL TO BUILD A CROSSING' and 'SAVE OUR CHILDREN'S LIVES'. Some of the children carried placards saying 'WE WANT A LOLLIPOP MAN'.

They plan to sit there every day between 9 o'clock and 4 o'clock until something's done.

Rates Rebels get Organized

Angry residents in Primrose Hill Coundon are up in arms. They're refusing to pay last month's Rates bills after an increase of over fifty-five percent on last year.

Mr Joseph Whitmarsh has been elected chairman of the Residents' Association. 'The increases are preposterous,' he said. 'Rates are already high in this area and we can see no good reasons for such massive increases. The Council has wasted public money and we're being made to foot the bill.'

The Primrose Hill residents are considering joining other dissatisfied rate-payers nationwide to press for rates reductions.

Mary Bristow, councillor for the area, is not very sympathetic. 'Of course, when the bill drops through the letter-box, it comes as a shock,' she said. 'But if you want a decent community with good amenities you have to pay for them. A cut in rates woud mean cuts in local authority spending on health services, education, sanitation, police and fire services.'

But the residents are adamant. They plan to withhold all payments until reductions are made.

Three accounts from the local newspaper about people who were prepared to take the law into their own hands. All of these activities, squatting, blocking the road and refusing to pay rates, are illegal. Sometimes, though, when everything fails, local people decide to use direct action to draw attention to their problem.

Many people argue that this is wrong. That the law is made to protect everybody and to keep some kind of order in society. If people are dissatisfied they should ask their members of parliament to change the laws. If they ignore the proper authorities and take part in illegal demonstrations then it's only one step away from revolution.

But what can ordinary citizens do if they object to something in their community? Or if the community doesn't provide something they want? What are the legal ways of changing things? What happens if the officials take no notice?

Look at the chart below. The circles show individuals and groups who have power to influence people or get things done in the local area. The squares show individuals and groups who have power and influence over the nation as a whole.

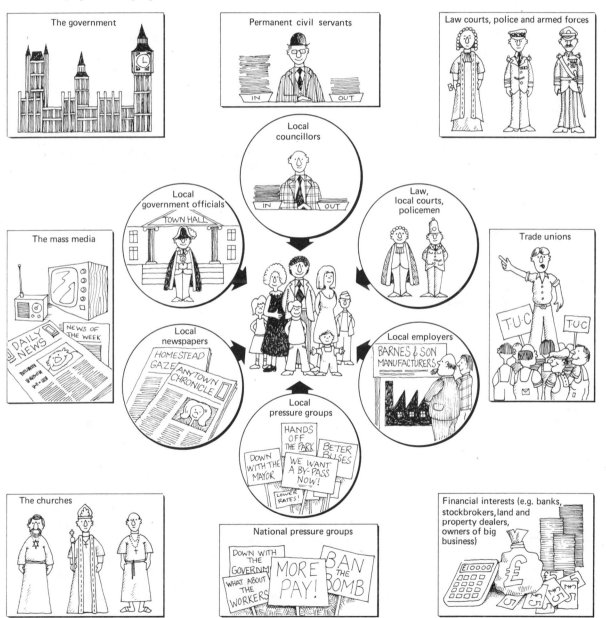

The government

Permanent civil servants

Law courts, police and armed forces

Local councillors

Local government officials

Law, local courts, policemen

The mass media

Trade unions

Local newspapers

Local employers

Local pressure groups

The churches

National pressure groups

Financial interests (e.g. banks, stockbrokers, land and property dealers, owners of big business)

Look at the chart on p.133.

1 Explain as fully as you can the meanings of the following terms: pressure group, local pressure group, national pressure group, local government officials, permanent civil servants, stock brokers, land and property dealers.

2 Explain the ways in which each of the groups shown have power or influence over ordinary people.
   Give examples wherever you can to illustrate your answer.

3 Which of a) the local groups, and b) the national groups, had the most power and which the least power over ordinary people? Be able to give reasons for your answer.

4 Do the members of these various groups have anything in common, e.g. a good education? Make a list of the things which people with power and influence have in common.

5 Which of the people in these groups are elected (i.e. voted for by ordinary people)? What happens to them if the people who elected them feel they're no longer representing their point of view?

6 Who appoints each of the individuals and groups who aren't elected by ordinary people?
   What happens to them if people disapprove of or disagree with what they do?

7 Find out about your local district councillor.
   a) What is his/her name?
   b) Which political party does he/she belong to?
   c) What are his/her main political interests? e.g. housing, education, the elderly etc.
   d) What decision-making committee does he/she belong to?
   e) Where could you get in touch with him/her if you want his/her help?
   f) How are district councillors elected?
   g) What's the difference between district councillors and county councillors?
   h) How are county councillors elected?
   i) What does the job of a councillor involve? How does it differ from that of a paid council official?

8 Find out about the local government officials in your area.
   a) Who is the Director of Education, the Director of Social Services, the Director of Finance, the Director of Housing, the Community Physician?
   b) What do their jobs involve?
   c) Who appoints them?
   d) Where and how do you get in touch with them if you need their help?

Look at the newspaper accounts on p. 132.

9 Explain as fully as you can what is meant by the following: squatting, compulsory purchase, rates, rate payers, local authority spending. Give examples or illustrations wherever this helps to make your definitions more clear.

10 Imagine you are Jim Henderson, unemployed fitter. You have nowhere to live and your family is split up.
   a) Write a letter to the Director of Housing explaining your problem and asking for his/her help.
   b) The Director of Housing tells you there is a big waiting list for council houses and there's nothing he/she can do.
      Write a letter to your local councillor explaining your problem and asking for his/her help.
   c) The councillor says he/she will mention your case to the Housing Committee but months pass and nothing happens. Write a letter to the local newspaper explaining your problem and complaining about the attitudes of the Director of Housing and the councillor.
   d) Your letter to the paper brings sympathetic replies from other homeless families and from Rick Davis the local organizer of Shelter.
      (i) Discuss together how you could use the following methods to publicize the problems of homeless people in your community, letters to the press, councillors and MPs, meetings with councillors and local officials, petitions, contacts with national newspapers and television, peaceful demonstrations, squatting.
      (ii) Produce some publicity handouts designed to get support from local people.
      (iii) Argue the rights and wrongs of deciding to squat.

11 Imagine you are Mrs Beaumont, organizer of NAG.
   a) How could you get evidence to prove to local officials that there is a lot of traffic in Norfolk Street?
   b) Explain why you decided to keep your child away from school and let him/her join you in a demonstration. Remember you are breaking the law and could be guilty of obstruction, public nuisance and refusing to send your child to school.
   c) Produce a publicity handout designed to get the support of local people for your demonstration.

12 a) Find out who in the community pays rates and how the money collected is spent. Who decides how it should be spent?
   b) Imagine that you are Joseph Whitmarsh and explain exactly why your Association objects to increased rates bills.

134

LOCAL INDUSTRY

Here's your chance to find out something about local industries. Make a list of the firms you know local people work in. Maybe, when you leave school, you're hoping to get a job in one yourself.

Divide into groups. Choose one of the firms and make as detailed and accurate a study as you can about the sort of place it is.

Here are some suggestions to help you.

BACKGROUND INFORMATION

1 Photograph or sketch the building of the firm you are studying and describe what it is like. Is it old? new? dilapidated? well-planned? Where is it situated?
2 Write a letter to the firm's information officer or personnel manager (in charge of appointing staff but also responsible for public relations). He/she will be able to send you leaflets about the firm or to answer individual questions.
   a) When was the firm established?
   b) Who owns it?
   c) Is it a local concern or are there branches in other parts of the country and the world?
   d) Who manages the firm?
   e) What kinds of things are produced?
   f) Where do the raw materials come from?
   g) Who buys the products made there?

VISIT

1 See if you can arrange to visit the firm you've chosen, if they can spare the time to show you round. This will give you a chance to ask more questions and to see inside. You should try to find out
   a) how many workers are employed (i) men? (ii) women?
   b) what kinds of jobs they do.
   c) if men and women do the same jobs.
   d) if men and women earn equal pay.
   e) what the wage rates are.
   f) if there is a union.
   g) what the facilities are like for meals, recreation, extra training and medical services in the firm.
   h) if there is a large turnover of workers. Why?

2 Describe some of the jobs you see being done.
   a) Are they being done by men or women?
   b) What does each job involve?
   c) Is it interesting? dangerous? boring?
   d) What are the workers' conditions like? clean? pleasant? noisy? dirty?
   e) Do the workers wear any protective clothing?
3 Arrange to interview the personnel manager.
   a) What is his/her view of the people who work there?
   b) What makes a good worker?
   c) Is the relationship between management and workers a good one?
   d) What happens if the workers have any complaints?
   e) Do they ever have any strikes?
   f) Do the workers get any perks?
   g) Do the workers receive sickness benefits, holiday pay, and pensions when they retire?
4 Arrange to interview the union representative.
   a) What is the name of the union?
   b) Do all the workers have to belong to the union?
   c) If there are women in the firm, do they
      (i) belong to the union?
      (ii) play leading parts in the union's activities?
   d) What are working conditions like?
   e) Is the union satisfied with the rates of pay?
   f) What are the relationships like between the management and the workers?
5 Try to talk to individual workers as you're going round the works or in the canteen.
   a) How long have they worked there?
   b) What do they think about the job?
   c) Do they know who owns the firm?
   d) Have they ever spoken to any of the managers?
   e) Do they know who their union representative is?
   f) Do they attend union meetings?
   g) Are there equal opportunities for men and women in the firm?
   h) Would they advise youngsters leaving school to join the firm?
   i) Do they get any perks working there?
   j) What do they like best about the job?
   k) What do they like least about the job?

FOLLOW—UP WORK

1 Produce an illustrated account of your visit to the firm and comment on what you found out. How did opinions of management, union and workers compare?
2 What are the effects of the firm, if any, on the surrounding community? Ask some of the people who live nearby what they think.
3 Would you like to work in the firm you studied? Give full reasons for your answer.

TALKING IT OVER

By now your group should have lots of information about one local firm. How does it compare with what other groups found out about their firms? It might be useful to let representatives from the firm you studied know what you think. Ask your teacher to arrange a meeting.

Invite some of the people you talked to, including local residents, to the school.

Let each group show their study and give a brief account of their findings.

This could lead to some searching questions and lively discussion.

'Put The Brakes On', Local Bike Workers Told

Workers in the Victoria-Brown bicycle factory were stunned by the news yesterday that their factory is to close. 'This is the first we'd heard of it,' said Freddie Nicholson, shop steward and worker in the factory for twenty years.

Sir Michael Brown, owner of the business, said that sales were falling every year and making bicycles was no longer profitable. He was sorry to see the firm close but it was better than bankruptcy.

The news has shocked the five hundred workers employed in Victoria-Browns. Many of them entered the trade as boys and have worked there all their lives. 'We'll never get jobs anywhere else in this town,' said William Burford, a fifty-five-year-old wheel-fitter. 'There's unemployment enough as it is and who'll take on someone my age?'

Asked about his plans Sir Michael said, 'I shall leave Coundon and retire to Scotland. I've had enough of work for one lifetime. I've put the premises on the market and I suppose it'll go to the highest bidder.'

What offers had Sir Michael had? 'Well there's a broiler company interested. You know, chickens and pigs, factory-farming I think they call it.'

The workers were less optimistic. 'It'll be the death of the community,' said Bert Andrews, a foreman in the plant. 'There's nothing else to do. Every family's got someone who works in Victoria's. It's like a household name in these parts.'

'I don't like the idea of broilers,' said Bill Finch, a twenty-five-year-old machine operator. 'There'll be no jobs for us in that. Anyway, you can't keep pigs and chickens in the middle of a town like this!'

Freddie Nicholson has demanded a meeting of all those concerned to talk the matter over. 'We're not just going to accept this,' he said. 'Our livelihood's at stake. We've got wives and kids to think of.'

Asked what he intended to do, he replied, 'We'll know better after the meeting. But I'm pushing for a 'work-in'. We'll buy the factory and run it ourselves.'

PROBLEM

What will be the effects on Coundon if Victoria-Brown closes? Could the workers run it themselves? Will the broiler company bring new jobs to the area? Should anything be done to persuade Sir Michael to change his mind?

There are lots of points of view to consider in a matter like this and many of them will be expressed in the public meeting. Here's how to argue it out for yourselves.

1 Arrange a meeting.
2 Give individual pupils roles to play (see pp. 137-8 for details). You will have to present your arguments clearly and do some research to make sure you get your facts right.
3 Those of you not playing key roles can be members of the Coundon community, anxious to ask questions and to decide which point of view to support. Try to really test the role players by asking awkward and difficult questions. This will mean some research on your part too.

THINGS TO FIND OUT

(It might be best for small groups of you to research one of these topics each and then report your findings to the rest of the class before the public meeting begins.)

1 Conduct a survey in your area to see if there is still a market for bicycles.
   a) How many adults have bicycles?

b) How many children have bicycles?

c) How many people use bicycles in preference to buses and cars for transport?

d) How many people use bicycles for leisure activities?

e) Have increased costs of cars and petrol made people return to using bikes?

2 Find out about other workers who have tried to run their factory themselves. Where did the money come from? Were they successful? What problems did they experience?

3 What is factory-farming really like? Arrange to visit a broiler house. What proportion of pigs and chickens are reared in this way? Do broiler houses pollute the environment with offensive smells? What is the view of a) the National Farmers Union? b) the Ministry of Agriculture? and c) the RSPCA on factory-farming?

4 How does it feel to be unemployed? Arrange to visit the local Unemployment Benefit Offices. Perhaps you could interview some people who are looking for jobs. What are the statistics of unemployment in your area? Which groups in the community are most affected? What benefits are unemployed workers and their families entitled to? What grievances have caused some unemployed workers to join the Claimants' Union?

5 Find out about the effects on other communities in Britain which have been seriously hit by unemployment, e.g. in Ulster, the Scottish Highlands and the north-east of England.

AUDIENCE QUESTIONS

(These are only a few suggestions. Work out others for yourself.)

a) to Arnold Elliot

'I've worked for five years at Victoria-Browns. Can I be sure I'll get a job in the broiler house?'

'How do the wages in the broiler house compare with ours?'

'What will you do to stop the smell of pigs getting into our homes?'

b) to Freddie Nicholson

'What experience have you got in running a business?'

'How will the "workers' control" be organized so that everyone gets a decent wage and a fair share of the profits?'

'Sir Michael says there's no market for bikes. Who are we going to sell them to?'

c) to Roger Morgan

'Are you prepared to support the decision taken by this meeting, even if you don't agree with it?'

'Will you ask the government to give us some money to get the 'work-in' started?'

THINGS TO DO

1 Write a letter to the 'Coundon Chronicle' as a local resident expressing your opinion about the threatened closure of the factory.

2 Having attended the meeting, write an account of what went on for the local newspaper.

ROLES

Alderman William Castle
Lord Mayor of Coundon. You act as chairman of the meeting and try to make sure that all sides get a fair hearing.

Sir Michael Brown
Owner of Victoria-Browns. You're sorry about the closure but have to look to your own financial interests.

Freddie Nicholson
Shop Steward. You think the workers should buy the factory and continue to run it themselves. You're convinced that there's still a market for your bikes and that you have the experience and workers to do the job.

Bill Finch
Machine operator. You're saving up to buy a house and you've got a young family to support. You and your wife were born and brought up in Coundon, all your relatives are here and you don't want to have to move somewhere else for work.

Bert Andrews
Foreman. You see the factory as a local concern. Many of the people who work here are related and they all live nearby. You think the community will die if the factory closes.

Amy Thomson
You have a husband and three married sons who all work for Victoria-Browns. Your whole family, including grandchildren, will be threatened if the factory closes.

Arnold Elliot
Broiler house owner and prospective buyer of the factory. You argue that you will spend money to modernize the plant and do all you can to prevent pollution. You cannot offer all the Victoria - Brown workers jobs but they will be given the first opportunities of work.

Mary Reynolds
You represent a group of women in East Anglia who organized a 'work-in' when their shoe factory was threatened with closure. You describe how you started making other leather and suede goods to keep yourselves in work, and succeeded.

Peter Brown
Son of Sir Michael Brown. You've studied economics at university and you think the family business is on the point of collapse, that the area is in decline and that your father should cut his losses and get out quickly.

David Armstrong
School teacher. You teach geography in the local school and know a bit about broiler houses. You argue that the smell of animal feed and excrement is disgusting and will pollute the whole area.

Marjorie Pringle
You represent RSPCA and you think that factory farming is cruel and immoral. You try to appeal to people's conscience and emotions.

Gus Major
You represent an American leisure company who'd be prepared to lend money to the workers if they could guarantee 'fun bikes' for export to the States.

Andrew Storey
Representative from the Ministry of Agriculture. You argue that we need to produce food cheaply and efficiently. You say that broiler houses are essential if the cost of food to housewives is to be kept down.

John Jarvis
Spokesman for the Claimants' Union. You give evidence about the 'raw deals' experienced by those families forced to rely on Welfare State benefits.

Councillor Arthur Terry
Local Liberal councillor. You say that bringing new industry to Coundon is a good thing. You argue that other industries should be encouraged to set up factories in the area.

Roger Morgan, MP
Labour MP for Coundon. You're anxious to prevent unemployment but you're doubtful about whether the workers can run their own factory. You advise them to seek jobs in the new broiler house.

Ellen Beaty
You live just across the road from the factory. You're anxious about the smells and fumes if the broiler house comes. It's not good for young children to grow up in polluted environments.

1 What is meant by the term 'community'?
2 Why are mining and trawling communities often very close-knit?
3 In what kind of areas would you expect to find middle-and upper-class communities?
4 What is the job of a Community Relations Officer?
5 What's the difference between prejudice and discrimination?
6 What is meant by people deciding to use 'direct action'?
7 What is the 'Director of Finance' responsible for in local government?
8 What are 'rates'?
9 What is the job of a 'personnel manager'?
10 What is meant by 'workers' control'?

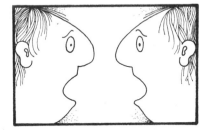

1 BILL   This life's a rat race. If I don't look after number one, nobody else will.

CHARLIE   Look pal, if you try to get more things than me and think you're better than me — that's suicide for our community. We should be working together not competing against each other.

BILL   What do you mean, work together? What about all the layabouts who do nothing? Should we work for them too?

CHARLIE   There are some people who can't support themselves in this world — either because they're too young or too old or too ill. Yeah — we should be responsible for them. They're part of our community aren't they? What if you got hurt at work tomorrow and could never earn wages again?

Bill and Charlie are discussing responsibilities in their community. Should they just be concerned about themselves or should they have concern for others?

a) Discuss together the pros and cons of each point of view, bringing in as many arguments as you can. Try to give examples and illustrations to support the arguments.
b) Divide into groups of two, each taking a different point of view. See how long you can keep Bill and Charlie's discussion going.
2 Imagine you are the leading spokesman at a local meeting. Choose a *real* problem in your own community (e.g. lack of nurseries for working mothers, not enough youth clubs, an inefficient local council, poor housing etc), and make a speech
a) describing the problem
b) offering suggestions for what should be done. You can use notes to help you but try not to read the speech. Do it 'off the cuff'.
3 Some people say that schools should belong to the community. They shouldn't be just for children, but for adults too. They should be open all day and until late at night for various activities. The local community should have a say in running them and influencing what goes on inside them. In some places community schools already exist.
a) How could ordinary schools change into community schools?
b) How could adults be encouraged to use the schools?
c) In what ways could the school help the community?
4 Invite a number of local people into your school to talk about their lives, jobs and responsibilities. Make a list of the people you'd like to hear from and some questions to ask them.

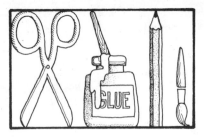

1

Find out all you can about the work of the Social Services Department of the local County Council. Who are their officials? What kinds of problems do they deal with? What action can they take?

2

Make a detailed study of your own community, including as many aspects of its life as you can. Make full use of photographs, interviews and survey techniques to illustrate your description and support your findings.

3

Make a study of a village community. Describe the occupations and social relationships of the village. How do the inhabitants react to newcomers? How has village life changed over the last thirty years?

4

Describe the activities and campaign of any local pressure group. What problem or grievance brought the group together? What methods do they use? How successful are they?

5

Find out all you can about the work, social life and community characteristics of either a mining area or a fishing community. What makes the community special?

6

Produce a project about the local newspaper or radio station in your area. Try to visit its offices and talk to some of its reporters or announcers and production team. Find out what their jobs involve. Describe each phase in the production of a daily paper or programme. What's good or bad about the finished product in your opinion? How is the paper or radio station financed? How does it compare with national papers or radio? Use cuttings and photos from the paper or recordings from the radio to illustrate your project.

7

Describe the work of the police in your community. How do they compare with TV policemen? Conduct a survey to test public attitudes to the police and police attitudes to the public. Comment particularly on their relationships with teenagers and immigrants.

9 PEOPLE WITH POWER

One of the most important things to understand when you're studying society is about power and influence. Who are the people with power in society? Who makes the decisions? Who influences what people think and do? Who benefits?

To have power and influence is to be able to affect other people's behaviour. If you can affect what another person does you have power. If you can't, you're powerless.

All of us have power and influence over somebody: a parent over a child, one friend over another, a teacher over a pupil. But some people in society have much more than others.

They have the power to affect the lives of vast numbers of people for good or ill.

Who are these people? Where does their power come from?

These are two of the questions we'll try to answer in this final chapter.

A panel of Labour MPs. From left to right: Michael Foot, Tony Benn, Peter Shore, Barbara Castle.

OUR MPs

In July 1975, MPs got their first pay increase for three and a half years to give them a salary of £5750 a year plus expenses. Not much compared to what other people with top professional jobs earn. But most of them earn money in other ways as well. In November 1975 the first *Register of MP's, Interests* was published listing each MP's other sources of income. Some were still practising journalists, solicitors or the directors of firms. Clement Freud, for example, Liberal MP for the Isle of Ely, besides being a business director, a journalist, a TV personality and an author, was also paid by a firm making dog-food for television commercials.

Some MPs argue that they have to take on other jobs to make ends meet. Others argue that MPs who accept money from other sources are either not giving their full attention to their jobs as an MP, or they are laying themselves open to charges of dishonesty. MPs who are in the pay of particular companies or who act as paid advisers (or consultants) to foreign governments may use their influence as MPs to get that company's or government's point of view over in parliament. This could be said to give those companies and governments an unfair advantage over their rivals.

Some MPs are members of trade unions. In the 1974 Labour government for example, twenty-nine MPs were sponsored by the engineering union and seventeen by the miners' union. All of them could use their power and influence as MPs to represent their unions as well as their constituents.

1 How are MPs elected and whom are they elected to represent?
2 Once elected, how much do they earn? How does this compare with the yearly salary of
   a) a headteacher of a secondary school?
   b) a bishop in the Church of England?
   c) a miner?
   d) an inspector in the police force?
   e) a bank manager?
3 What extra allowances are MPs entitled to on top of their salary? Do you think MPs are well paid or poorly paid for the jobs they do? Give reasons for your answer.
4 What is the yearly salary of
   a) the prime minister?
   b) a cabinet minister?
   c) the leader of the opposition?
   d) a member of the shadow cabinet?
5 Do you think it matters that many MPs do other jobs like journalism or being a lawyer as well as being an MP? Give full reasons for your answer.
6 a) Explain what is meant by a 'consultant'.
   b) Suggest some of the possible dangers of MPs who act as 'consultants' or who are paid by business and financial interests, as advisers or company directors.
7 Explain what is meant by a trade union 'sponsoring' an MP. Suggest some of the possible dangers of MPs being sponsored by trade unions.

THE SOCIAL CLASS OF MPs

Members of parliament, although representing the country as a whole, are more likely to come from the upper and middle classes than the working class. The party with the largest number of working-class MPs is the Labour Party, but even here, the number of middle-class MPs increase year by year. These figures are for 1966. Today there are even fewer working-class MPs.

1 a) Make a list of the characteristics of middle-class people and their way of life which might help and encourage them to become MPs.
   b) Make a list of the characteristics of working-class people and their way of life which might make it difficult for them to become MPs.
   c) Make a list of influences in society which might make it easier for middle-class people to become MPs than working-class people.
2 Look at table 1. Why are the workers who become MPs more likely to represent the Labour Party than the Conservative or Liberal Parties?
3 Since the middle class make up only about one third of the population,
   a) Do you think it's fair that the majority of MPs are middle class?
   b) Do you think that middle-class people are capable of representing the interests of working-class people?
   Give full reasons for your answers.
4 Look at tables 2a and 2b.
   a) What is a public school?
   b) Work out what percentage of Conservative MPs and Labour MPs in the 1974 parliament had been to public schools. Which is greater? Suggest reasons why.
   c) Three-quarters of Conservative MPs and five-eighths of Labour MPs in the 1974 parliament had been to university. Suggest reasons why Conservative M Ps were more likely to have been to Oxford or Cambridge and Labour MPs to universities other than Oxford or Cambridge.

Table 1
Occupation of Members of Parliament

	Conservative	Labour	Liberal
Professions (e.g. lawyers, accountants)	117	156	6
Businessmen	75	32	3
Miscellaneous (e.g. journalists, farmers etc)	59	66	3
Workers (e.g. miners, electricians)	1	109	
Total	235	363	12

(Source: R. Rose, *Politics in England*)

Table 2a
The Education of MPs (1974)

SCHOOLS	Conservative	Labour	Liberal
Eton	48	1	2
Harrow	10		
Other Public Schools	116	24	3
Total	174	25	5
Total Number of MPs	276	319	13

(Source: *The Times Guide to the House of Commons*)

Table 2b

UNIVERSITIES	Conservative	Labour	Liberal
Oxford	80	60	3
Cambridge	73	24	2
Other Universities	56	106	2
Total	209	190	7
Total Number of MPs	276	319	13

(Source: *The Times Guide to the House of Commons*)

An MP's life is hard, the pay is poor, the hours are long - but oh!, the breathtaking feeling of power.

Table 3a   *GENERAL ELECTIONS 1974*   Seats won by the parties

February 1974

Party	Seats
Labour	301
Conservative	296
Liberal	14
Scottish Nationalist	7
United Ulster Unionist	11
Plaid Cymru (Welsh Nationalist)	2
Social Democratic & Labour (N. Ireland)	1
Democratic Labour Independent Labour (N. Ireland)	1
The Speaker	1
	635

October 1974

Party	Seats
Labour	319
Conservative	276
Liberal	13
Scottish Nationalist	11
United Ulster Unionist	10
Plaid Cymru (Welsh Nationalist)	2
Social Democratic & Labour (N. Ireland)	1
Independent Labour (N. Ireland)	1
The Speaker	1
	635

Table 3b *Votes Cast For the Parties*

Votes Cast February 1974

Party	Votes	Percentage of Votes Cast
Labour	11 654 726	37.2
Conservative	11 963 207	38.2
Liberal	6 063 470	19.3
Others	1 651 823	5.3

Votes Cast October 1974

Party	Votes	Percentage of Votes Cast
Labour	11 447 165	39.3
Conservative	10 458 548	35.8
Liberal	5 348 193	18.3
Others	1 920 534	6.6

VOTE! VOTE! VOTE!

1 a) Make a list of the things that people take into account when voting for an MP.
   b) Ask a group of voters to rearrange the list into their order of importance.
   c) Which three things did the people you interviewed think were the most important to take into account when voting for an MP?
2 a) Ask the following questions of as many people in as many of these different groups as you can: school pupils, teachers, factory-workers, house-wives, old-age pensioners, policemen, owners of small businesses, members of the armed forces: If there was a general election tomorrow, which political party would you vote for if you could? Why?

b) Produce a number of bar charts like the one here to show the way the people in each group would vote.

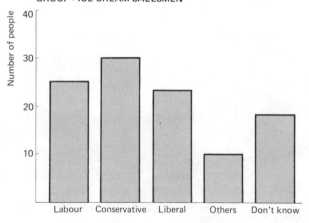

GROUP : ICE CREAM SALESMEN

c) Which groups would be most likely to vote Labour and Conservative according to your survey?

Write a report to comment on the main reasons given by each group for voting for a particular party.

3   Look carefully at tables 3a and 3b.
Find out the reasons why
a) The Labour Party won the election of February 1974 even though they were given fewer votes than the Conservative Party.
b) The Liberal Party had 18.3% of the votes cast in October 1974 but only thirteen MPs, whilst the others had 6.6% of the votes cast and twenty-six MPs.
c) What is the job of the Speaker? Who is the present Speaker in the House of Commons? Is he an MP? How is he chosen?

FIRST IMPRESSIONS

My first impressions of the House of Commons were of a kind of living museum. The Speaker was dressed as he would have been in the eighteenth century, the Serjeant-at-Arms and his deputies were also in antique dress, and in the members' cloakroom, beneath each hook, a loop of pink ribbon was religiously renewed whenever it faded, for each member to hang up his sword!

Nearly everything is connected with tradition. I learnt that while it is correct to refer to members of the same party as 'Honourable Friends', those on the other side are, normally 'Right Honourable Friends' 'Gentlemen', or 'Members', according to whether they sit on the same or opposite side of the House. Retired Officers of the armed forces are 'Right Honourable and Gallant'. Lawyers are 'Right Honourable and Learned'.

Stan Newens
Labour MP for Harlow

Peers are 'Noble Lords'. And you're supposed to refer to members' constituencies too. For example, my 'Honourable Friend the member for Kingston upon Hull East'.

I was surprised to find that heckling and jeering in the House are quite common. Shortly after I first arrived, one of Harold Wilson's speeches was made almost completely inaudible by the noise from the Conservative benches. Seeing a piece of paper being passed from hand to hand on the other side of the House, I enquired, amid the hubbub, what was going on. The MP next to me explained that it was probably instructions for everyone to talk and to create such a row that Wilson wouldn't be heard. 'Disgraceful,' I commented in anger. 'If only the Public could see this!'

'Don't get so excited,' my colleague replied. 'After all we do it to them as well!'

I soon learned that shouting out is traditional in the House. 'Answer', is shouted when speakers try to evade questions. 'Sit down', if somebody with whom you disagree is trying to intervene when a speaker from the front benches is speaking. 'Rubbish', and 'Disgrace', when things you disagree with are being said by the other side.

Amidst all this tomfoolery the Speaker has to try to keep order and is continually reprimanding the members for their flippant and school-boy-like behaviour.

CONSTITUENCY WORK

Most of my work isn't done at the House at all but in my constituency. I am a kind of local ombudsman, to whom all and sundry come when they are in difficulties, with government offices, local authorities, the police, the Inland Revenue, their own relatives or anyone else.

If a constituent is unable to obtain a house, if he has been refused a pension, if his neighbours' teenage son is taking potshots at the washing on the line in his garden with an air gun, he comes to me. I am deluged the whole year through with a range of problems which concern almost every aspect of life, from the most public to the most intimate of issues.

On the first Saturday of every month I have an advice bureau. A steady stream of constituents keeps me busy from 9 a.m. to about 7 p.m. Every day I receive about twenty letters. I am telephoned at home at all hours of the day and throughout the weekend. I am never without some work waiting to be done.

Some of the problems are hardly those you would expect an MP to tackle. I have been asked to pursue a missing letter, to deal with the problems of burst pipes, to take action about the wallpaper being used by Council decorators, and even to help a man who thought his brain was being controlled by a transmitter in outer space. The case of a lady who lost her false teeth whilst being sick involved me in a long correspondence with the National Health Service about getting them replaced!

POSTSCRIPT

The work of an MP is hard and never-ending. The pressure is such that I never have time to read books, study the news or see television programmes as I did in the past. It would be very easy to lose sight of the original reasons which led me into the Labour party — the need for fundamental social changes to make a fairer Britain for all. Now that I have the opportunity to meet my political opponents face to face, I find many of them to be likeable and humane people of the highest principles. The atmosphere of the bars, which don't keep normal licensing hours, the dinners and social functions which cut across party lines all tend to blur the differences of principle with genuine ties of friendship and respect.

At the same time, it's easy to become cut off from your roots. Evenings are spent in the House or at meetings and social functions. Less and less time is available for meeting with and talking to ordinary people. I feel drawn away from the working-class background of my past.

Compromise — the toning down of extreme points of view — seems much more reasonable than before. It's easy to conclude that class barriers are a figment of the imagination of the immature and those with a grievance, and to fit cosily into your new environment.

But, frustrated as I am, I still believe that my work as an MP is worthwhile. Whenever I'm asked, I'm reluctant to concede that I enjoy being in parliament. But for the present, I'm glad to be there and intend in the future to do all I can to remain there.

(Adapted from *Work 2,* ed. Ronald Fraser when Stan Newens was MP for Epping)

Read Stan Newens' account of entering parliament as an MP and then try these questions:

1 a) Explain as fully as you can why Stan Newens thought the House of Commons was like a 'living museum'.
   b) What does he mean by 'I'm a kind of local ombudsman'?
   c) Why does he find it difficult to remain true to his background, the people he represents and his political principles?

2 Find out and explain the meanings of each of the following parliamentary terms:
   the back benches, the front benches, the cabinet, the shadow cabinet. Her Majesty's opposition, the privy council, the other side of the House, party whips.

3 If you were an MP, what would be the correct way of addressing
   a) a lady lawyer in your own party?
   b) a shadow minister?

4 a) What is meant by the term constituency?
   b) Who is the MP for your constituency?
   c) Which political party does he/she represent?

5 Write a letter to your local MP or ask your teacher to arrange for him/her or one of his/her helpers to come and talk to you.
   a) When and how could you get in touch with your MP if you needed help?
   d) What was his/her job before becoming an MP?
   e) Where was he/she educated?
   f) Is he/she a member of trade union?
   g) Does he/she do any other job besides being an MP?
   h) Does he/she have any special responsibilities in parliament?
   i) Is he/she a member of the front benches or the back benches, the government or the opposition?

6 How much power do MPs have to influence the type of laws which are passed in parliament? Find out
   a) how a bill becomes a law.
   b) how much influence the party whips have on the way MPs vote.
   c) what happens if an MP votes against the policy of his/her party.

The Labour Party,	The Liberal Party,
Transport House,	National Liberal Club,
Smith Square,	1 Whitehall Place,
London SW1.	London SW1

The Conservative Party,
Conservative & Unionist Association,
32, Smith Square,
London SW1.

These are the London addresses of the three main political parties. There will also be local branches in your area. Write a letter to each of them and find out the answers which will help you to complete the chart opposite.(If you live in Northern Ireland, Scotland or Wales, add the Ulster Unionists, the Scottish Nationalists or the Welsh Nationalists to your chart.)

Party attitudes to each of the following issues.			
	Labour	Conservative	Liberal
Secondary Schools			
Nationalization			
North Sea Oil			
Abortion			
Spending on Defence			
Trade Unions			
Income Tax			
Private Medicine			
Council Housing			
Prices & Wages			
Separate parliaments for N. Ireland Wales and Scotland			

THE UNIONS

When some people talk of trade unions these days — 'communists', 'greed', 'blackmail' and 'holding the country to ransom' are their favourite descriptions. A young clerical worker interviewed for the *Observer* said, 'Money has no value to miners as it has to other people; they only spend it on beer.' He was studying to be an accountant at night school and reckoned that at the end of four years he would have earned his money. 'If you're studying for years to be a surgeon or something, you deserve more. It's the communists among the miners trying to bring the country down.'

Is he right? Are the trade unions too powerful? A lot of people think they are. Others argue that they need to be in order to protect the interests of working people against employers, share-holders eager to make profits and politicians who try to exploit them.

CONFRONTATION

During the sixties unions became more powerful. The numbers of people joining them increased, but as

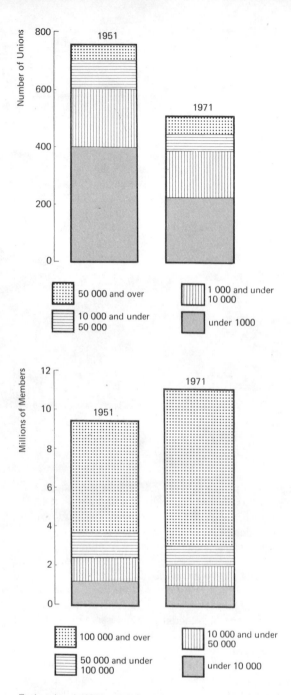

Number of Unions

1951

1971

- ▦ 50 000 and over
- ⊟ 10 000 and under 50 000
- ▥ 1 000 and under 10 000
- ▨ under 1000

Millions of Members

1951

1971

- ▦ 100 000 and over
- ⊟ 50 000 and under 100 000
- ▥ 10 000 and under 50 000
- ▨ under 10 000

Trade unions in 1951 and 1971:
number of unions and number of members.

these charts show, the number of different unions grew less. Now more than half of all trade members belonged to one of nine big unions.

Strikes about pay and working conditions also increased but conflict between the unions and the government came to a head after 1971 when the Conservative Government passed the Industrial Relations Act. The Act, among other things, was an attempt to control the workers' right to strike and tried to impose heavy fines on unions which broke the law. This act together with inflation (rapidly rising prices and a fall in the value of money) and fears of unemployment led the unions to wage war on the Conservative Government. The miners played a leading part in this.

Their wages were low in 1973. Most people agreed that they were a special case and deserved big pay increases. Their strike lasted several weeks and forced the government to give in to their demands.

In 1974 the miners went on strike again. The Conservative Government vowed that it would not give in again. In an attempt to save fuel and electricity, the government declared 'a state of national emergency', putting most workers in the country on a three-day week. Other unions supported the miners. To them the battle was about more than wages. It was about a government which they believed was opposed to working people. The government argued that 'militant trades unionists weren't representative of the country as a whole'. The press spread rumours about 'communist inspired plots'. Ordinary people suffered — as much from the stubbornness of the government as anything else.

In February the prime minister, Edward Heath, called a general election, asking for public support to beat the unions. He lost by a narrow majority. The Labour party came back to power, gave the miners another pay increase and within a few weeks had fulfilled their election promise to 'get the country back to work'.

This was a power which unions, in all their long history, had never equalled. The power to bring down a government they disapproved of and replace it by one they wanted. It was widely believed in 1974 that it was the miners who had beaten the Conservatives, not the Labour party.

1 a) Who are the present leaders of the following
      unions?
      Amalgamated Union of Engineering Workers,
      Transport and General Workers Union,
      National Union of Miners,
      National Union of Railwaymen,
      Union of Post Office Workers,
      Association of Scientific, Technical and
      Managerial Staffs,
      National Union of General Municipal Workers,
      National Union of Teachers,
      National Association of Local Government
      Officers.
   b) Which of these could be called 'general unions'?
      Which of them 'industrial unions'?
      And which of them 'white-collar unions'?
2 Ask your teacher to arrange for the local
   representatives of some trade unions to come and
   talk to you.
   Use the opportunity to find out:
   how unions are organized locally and nationally.
   why workers should belong to trade unions.
   how shop stewards are appointed.
   how decisions are taken locally and nationally.
   the difference between official and unofficial strikes.
   some of the reasons which cause trade union
   members to go on strike.
   what part women workers play in the union.
   what part young people play in the union.
   what influence trade unions have on politicians.
   what their answer would be to members of the
   public who accuse them of being 'communist
   inspired', 'greedy' and 'holding the country
   to ransom'.
3 Labour and Conservative governments over the last
   ten years have tried various ways of controlling the
   power of the unions. Explain carefully each of
   these approaches, describing how they differed from
   each other and how successful they were.
   a) In Place of Strife.
   b) The Industrial Relations Act.
   c) The Social Contract.
4 Explain as accurately as you can the present
   relationship between the government and the trade
   unions. Use newspaper cuttings to illustrate your
   answer.

For help in answering this section write to the Trades
Union Congress (see p. 160).

THE PRESS

In 1974 there were nine national daily and seven Sunday
newspapers. But there were also over a hundred local
papers published each day and about a thousand more
each week. This sounds like a lot for the public to choose
from, and an opportunity to read many different points
of view. But what sometimes isn't realized is that most of
these newspapers were owned by the same people. The
four biggest newspaper publishers, IPC, News International
Limited, Beaverbrook Newspapers and the Thomson
Organization owned between them the best-selling national
newspapers, most of the local newspapers, and scores of
weekly and monthly magazines.

TITLE	CONTROLLED BY	CIRCULATION (1974)
Dailies		
EXPRESS	Beaverbrook Newspapers Ltd.	3 226 936
MAIL	Associated Newspapers Ltd.	1 768 207
MIRROR	IPC	4 192 491
TELEGRAPH	Daily Telegraph Ltd.	1 427 439
FINANCIAL TIMES	Pearson Longman Ltd.	198 574
THE GUARDIAN	Guardian Newspapers Ltd.	364 635
MORNING STAR	People's Press Printing Society	49 842
SUN	News International Ltd.	3 302 996
THE TIMES	The Thomson Organisation	351 205
Sundays		
NEWS OF THE WORLD	News International Ltd.	5 872 028
OBSERVER	Observer Trust	832 983
SUNDAY PEOPLE	IPC	4 386 861
SUNDAY EXPRESS	Beaverbrook Newspapers Ltd.	4 059 983
SUNDAY MIRROR	IPC	4 570 712
SUNDAY TELEGRAPH	Daily Telegraph Ltd.	776 783
SUNDAY TIMES	The Thomson Organisation	1 505 385

This chart shows the ownership and circulation figures of national newspapers in 1974.

THE POWER OF THE PRESS

Newspapers like to claim that they're 'the guardians of the public interest'. Their critics often accuse them of being controlled by the wealthy for their own ends. The truth probably lies somewhere between the two.

Over the years three powerful forces have shaped the press in Britain — politicians, business interests and advertising.

BUSINESS INTERESTS

Business and financial interests often use the press for their own ends. Lavish luncheons to which the press are invited are usually followed by favourable 'facts' being reported in the next issues of the newspapers. On the other hand, reports in the press about internal arguments or financial troubles can have disastrous effects on business interests. The value of a company's shares may be reduced by unfavourable press reports. So like the politicians, businessmen have become expert at keeping certain information secret and feeding the press the information they want publicized.

ADVERTISING

Money from advertising provides most of the cash to produce newspapers. Without advertising the cost of the *Daily Mirror* would increase four-fold and the *Daily Telegraph* eight-fold. Without advertising most newspapers would soon go out of business.

Recently a leading supermarket chain was fined in the High Court for charging more than the proper price for products marked '3p off'. Information about the supermarket's criminal and unfair behaviour was hardly mentioned in the press. It was suggested by some critics that this was because the supermarket threatened to withdraw its advertising contract from newspapers which gave it bad publicity.

Advertising also has a big influence on the style and approach of newspapers, especially the popular dailies like the *Sun*, the *Mirror*, the *Express* and the *Mail*. Advertisers are interested in buying the attention of the maximum number of people. If a paper is read by a lot of people, it can charge thousands of pounds for advertising space. This encourages some newspapers to cater for a mass audience. In the popular dailies this means mixing news with entertainment and concentrating on human-interest stories, gossip, sex, crime and sport.

POLITICIANS

Politicians like to feed the press with information they want publicized. But there are some things which they'd rather keep secret from the public and which they don't want the press to find out about. Pressmen call this the 'real news' and compete with each other to get hold of it. For this reason laws have been introduced to keep a good many government discussions secret. Discussions in cabinet, for instance, are not allowed to be published for thirty years.

Most of the political news in papers though, is about things which politicians want the press to publish, either because it's in their favour, or because it's against their opponents. This article from the *Sunday Express*, for example, gives a good deal of free publicity to Mrs Thatcher and the Conservatives.

HE WOMAN WHO COULD LEAD BRITAIN

was a street corner shop, a grocer's stores. A place with its wn distinctive aroma blended from coffee, spices, and sides of con.

Its proprietor, Mr Roberts, was a considerable figure in the wn: a member of the council, a lay preacher and school gover- r. A man whose creed was integrity, independence and hard rk.

Altogether, Roberts' Stores was a bit more than a shop. It was mething of a local institution.

Sometimes customers were served by Mr Roberts' daughters, uriel and Margaret. Both of them have vivid and happy emories of the shop and of the home above it.

Today, one of them is a farmer's wife.

The other could well be the next occupant of No. 10 wning Street.

In 1951 Margaret Roberts became Mrs Thatcher. In 1959 e became a Member of Parliament. In February of this year, ter a fierce struggle in the Tory Party, she became Leader of e Opposition.

Mrs Thatcher's bid for the leadership was a gamble. Had she st, her career could well have come to a full stop. But she took e calculated risk and won.

How has it come about that a grocer's daughter now heads e party that is traditionally associated with the aristocracy and g business?

Mrs Thatcher has given a clue. She was greatly influenced by r father. She has absorbed his precepts. She recalls: 'In our usehold you did not sit idle. It was very much the Parable of e Talents. If you had ability, it was a heinous sin to dig it into e ground. It was your duty to better your lot by your own forts.'

The progress of Margaret Thatcher, from her early days in e shop at Grantham, to her battle for the Tory leadership has en traced in detail by *Sunday Express* writer Geoffrey Park- use.

He has talked to people who knew her at school, and at iversity; to those who watched her first unsuccessful attempts obtain a parliamentary seat; to those who have been close to r throughout her political career.

An intriguing picture emerges.

Margaret Thatcher has never been Britain's most popular litician. Her career has had set-backs. She has been vilified by r opponents, and has sometimes received less than rapture om members of her own party.

But a pattern is discernible. At every stage in her career, she s set herself targets — and she has attained them.

Now one target remains...

The life-story of Mrs Margaret Thatcher begins next week in e *Sunday Express.*

Most newspapers are known to favour one party more than another and this obviously affects the way they report the news stories about them.

What the papers say:

1 Explain carefully what is meant by a newspaper's 'circulation'.
2. Make a collection of different national newspapers for the same day of the week.

a) Which daily newspaper has the biggest circulation and which the smallest? From looking at copies of these newspapers, suggest reasons for their big or small circulations.

b) Some of them are called 'quality' papers and others 'popular' papers. Explain which you think are 'popular' and which 'quality'. Give reasons for your answer.

c) What do you immediately notice about
   (i)   the presentation and layout of different papers?
   (ii)   the size of the print?
   (iii) the contents of the paper?
   (iv)   the number of pictures?

d) Make a note of the main headlines in each paper. What do you notice about them?

e) What are the main news stories in each paper? How much space does each paper give to the main stories? (Count the number of columns and measure the amount of type in inches).

f) Read an account of the same event in each of the papers.
   (i)   Do the facts vary in any of the papers?
   (ii)   How does the style of reporting differ in 'popular' and 'quality' papers?
   (iii) Can you tell whether the paper is on one side or another in its attitude to the news story?

g) Study the adverts in the 'popular' and 'quality' press. Which papers have most adverts? Do you notice any differences in the kinds of adverts in different papers?

h) Which papers try to be most entertaining in your opinion? Give examples of how they do this. Explain whether you think this makes them better newspapers or worse.

i) Explain what is meant by each of the following:
   (i)   human-interest stories.
   (ii)   cheque-book journalism.
   (iii) gutter press.
   (iv)   'exclusive' stories.
   (v)   sledge-hammer headlines.

Can you find examples of any of these in your collection of newspapers?

j) Find stories about leading politicians in different papers.
   (i)   Are they being given good publicity?
   (ii) Are they being made fun of in any kindly or unkind way?
   (iii) Are their policies or personalities being criticized?
   (iv) Can you tell whether the newspaper favours one politician and political party rather than another?
   (v)   What influence might these stories have on people who read them?

k) Find examples of business or financial interests getting either good or bad publicity in different newspapers.

3 a) Suggest which newspapers you think are most likely to be read by middle-class people and which by working-class people.

b) Conduct a small survey among teachers (who could be said to be middle class) and factory workers (who could be said to be working class) to see if you're right.

c) Suggest reasons why middle-class and working-class people in general tend to read different newspapers.

4 Find out who owns the local newspapers in your area. Do they belong to any of the big four publishing companies?
Arrange with your teacher to visit the local newspaper offices to see how a paper is produced.

5 Make a list of six popular magazines. Find out who owns them.

6 Write a paragraph to explain why you think newspapers have power and influence in society. Give examples to support your argument.

7 Working in small groups or as a class, produce a newspaper of your own. Make it full of local news, interviews and adverts for social happenings — in fact all the day-to-day activities which people in the area will be interested to read about. Your earlier study of national newspapers should give you some ideas about the best approaches to take.

TELE-POWER

On 17 July 1975 an incredible scientific achievement was seen by millions of people all over the world. American astronauts and Russian cosmonauts shook hands in space. After two separate launchings, Soyuz in Russia and Apollo in America, the space ships were joined together in space, and their passengers were able to visit each others' space ship. Such an achievement would have been hard to believe if we hadn't seen it with our own eyes. Even more incredible than this amazing feat was the fact that millions of people all over the world watched every detail of the space journey while it actually happened.

This is just one reason why television is so important. No longer do we need to rely solely on people telling us what's happening, or to read books and newspapers to find out about things. Because of live television we can see for ourselves. We can be much more knowledgeable about what's going on in the world than ever before.

But not all television programmes are 'live'. Most programmes are made beforehand and are edited and put together from a good deal more film and video tape than we ever see in the finished product. In deciding which bits of film to show and which to leave out it's possible for bias to creep in. The viewers don't get the whole story. They only get the film-maker's or the reporter's interpretation of it. His/her version may be very accurate, but it may also be one-sided.

Just like the press, a good deal of television is what 'some' people want the 'rest of us' to see.

TELEVISION HISTORY

You probably take television for granted and forget to be impressed by it. But you don't need to be very old to remember a time before every household had a television. True, television was invented in the 1920s by a Scotsman, John Logie Baird, and the BBC, the world's first television service, began broadcasting in 1936. But when broadcasting was resumed after the war only about 20 000 homes had their own sets.

It wasn't until the 1950s that the television craze began to spread throughout the country, encouraged by the coverage given to the Coronation of Queen Elizabeth II in 1953. At first people distrusted its safety and novelty but it soon became a status symbol and won pride of place in thousands of living-rooms.

At first there was only one channel but commercial television was established in 1954 and BBC 2 in 1964. In 1967 BBC 2 began to transmit programmes in colour and by 1970 more than eighty-five per cent of the homes in Britain had television sets. By 1975 over half of these were colour televisions.

HOW TELEVISION IS FINANCED

1975-6		
£ 213 million from licences £ 3 million from Open University £0.15 million from sale of publications etc.		BBC TV & radio
£ 152 million from advertising (after paying £22 million levy to the government and £14½ million to the IBA for renting programme time)		ITV

Proportion of the time given to ITV programmes (IBA 1973)

1 How are the BBC and the IBA financed?
2 Although they are given a good deal of freedom, both the BBC and the IBA are responsible to parliament. They both must agree to provide programmes which are 'informative, educational and entertaining'. What are they not allowed to do?

3 a) Make a list of the fifteen regional companies which make up Independent Television.
   b) Which ITV company operates in your area?
4 'ITV is more concerned to reach a mass-audience than the BBC.' This statement is probably true. Can you suggest why?
5 Television has both its defenders and its critics. Here are their main arguments.

CRITICS SAY	DEFENDERS SAY
Television is guilty of distortion and of deliberately misleading the viewers by withholding information, lying, exaggerating, or giving only half-truths, especially in advertising.	Live television can let people see what's going on in the world while it's actually happening.
The vivid presentation of sex, crime and violence encourages permissive, criminal and violent behaviour in the viewers.	Television is educational. In the comfort of their own living rooms people can learn more about other countries, art, history, literature, science and politics than they ever did at school.
Swearing and vulgarity in plays and comedy shows has a bad influence on viewers.	Television can provide the best in entertainment: music, drama, films and variety with top stars and talented performers in people's own home.
People watch too much television. Their minds become dull and they lose the capacity to think for themselves.	Through watching television people become interested in sports like show-jumping, golf and athletics which they might otherwise have known nothing about.
Advertising distorts the facts and makes consumers greedy for material possessions.	Because of television, the general public is well informed about the issues of the day. This can be seen at election time.
Television is used by politicians and businessmen to extend their power and influence over ordinary people.	

---

a) Discuss each argument together. How far do you agree or disagree with it?
b) Can you find any evidence from sociological research to support or reject any of these arguments?
c) Add other arguments of your own for or against television to these lists.

6 It is said that the middle class is more likely to watch BBC 1 and BBC 2, and the working class is more likely to watch ITV.
   a) Conduct a small survey among teachers (who could be said to be middle class) and factory workers (who could said to be working class) to see if this is true.
   b) What are the three most favourite programmes of each group in your sample?
   c) Write a report to show whether you found any differences between middle-class and working-class viewing habits and suggest reasons to explain your findings.

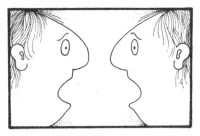

1 When was a *Register of MPs' Interests* published for the first time?
2 What information did the *Register* give?
3 Which political party is most likely to get support from the trade unions?
4 Name three of the minor parties who took part in the 1974 general elections.
5 What is the job of the Speaker in the House of Commons?
6 What is the job of the party whips in the House of Commons?
7 Which government was responsible for the Industrial Relations Act?
8 Which British prime minister declared a state of national emergency and lost an election because of the miners' strike in 1974?
9 Which Sunday newspaper had the largest circulation in 1974?
10 When was Independent Television established?

Speakers' Corner in Hyde Park: one of the most famous places in the world for standing on a soap box, putting up banners and declaring your point of view to anyone who'll listen.

As long as you're not too obscene, you don't tell damaging lies about someone, and you don't act in a way that's likely to cause a 'breach of peace', you can say whatever you like – something people in Britain rather proudly refer to as 'freedom of speech'.

People at Speakers' Corner talk about anything and everything, from the second coming of Jesus Christ to performing yoga. But most of the issues have something to do with power and politics.

Here are a list of titles. You can add others of your own. Choose one of them and make a speech lasting about five minutes – as if you were at Speakers' Corner.

Don't forget that the people in the audience have the right to ask you difficult questions. A good speaker should be able to answer in an amusing and intelligent way.

'Social-class barriers are breaking down.'
'The rich get richer and the poor get poorer.'
'Money can't buy you love.'
'Public schools should be abolished.'
'There should be more women MPs.'
'The monarchy should be abolished.'
'The Queen should run the country.'
'Home rule for Ireland, Scotland and Wales.'
'MPs' other incomes.'
'Why we need the unions.'
'Why we don't need the unions.'
'Support our strike.'
'Censor the press.'
'Clean up television.'

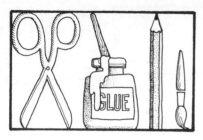

1

Write the life history of a man or woman who you think has had a powerful influence on other people.

2

Write a report on the lives of people who, in an affluent society, still live below the Official Poverty Line. What does poverty mean to these people? Why does our society allow such hardships to continue? Contact the National Children's Bureau, 8 Wakley Street, London EC1V 7QE, the Child Poverty Action Group, 1 Macklin Street, Drury Lane, London WC2 and your Local Authority's Social Services Department for more information.

3

What is one of the biggest political issues of the day? Describe it carefully and then collect information to illustrate the points of view of all the main political parties. After comparing their arguments and looking at the evidence, say which point of view you support.

4

Make a study of the most recent general election, local by-election or local council election in your area. Who were the different candidates? What were their policies? How did they get publicity for themselves? How did they try to persuade people to vote for them? Who was successful? Include press reports, campaign stickers and manifestos if possible.

5

Make a study of either the Dockers' or one of the Railwaymen's Unions. Show their early struggles for recognition, the problem they had to overcome, some important dates in their history, their strength today. Describe how the conditions of work in their industry have changed over the years.

6

Cartoons are frequently used in the press to make fun of politicians or to make an important comment on a current political issue. Draw your own political cartoons.

"Well, that gets you into Rhodesia, Carver—now what's your plan for meeting S₁

7

The car industry is infamous for its bad relationships between management and workers. Strikes are common. Can you explain why? What is there about working in the car industry which creates such problems?

Try to visit one or arrange for union and management representatives to come and talk to you.

8

Make a survey of public attitudes to trade unions. Write a report to describe your findings.

11

Make a study of selected BBC or ITV programmes for a week. Show what proportion of them fall into each of the categories shown on p.153.

13

Pretend that you're a television critic for the *Daily Rag*. Write comments on the programmes you saw last night in the style of a newspaper report.

9

Choose one leading politician and collect newspaper stories about him/her over a period of a few weeks. Which details do the papers seem most interested in — political or personal? Is the politician mainly supported or criticized by the press? What 'type of person' does the politician seem to be, according to the press? What 'official information' about the politician can you find out by writing to party headquarters?

Write a letter to the politician or to his/her party, quoting some of the comments from the press. What does he/she, or they think about them?

12

What is your favourite television programme? Find out as much as you can about how it's made, who produces it, the people who appear in it. Why is it your favourite?

14

Try to find out how much different companies pay to advertise their products in the local press, the national press and on television. How do they justify spending so much money?

10

Make a collection of newspaper stories about sex, crime and violence. Write a critical account of whether you think this is good or bad reporting and why.

Soho sex films face GLC ban

Flight to freedom from a Japanese jail

'Loophole' killed addict heiress

My mad scene

INDEX

GLOSSARY

ATTITUDE   Way of thinking.
BAR CHART   A diagram to show
the relationship between
different figures or statistics.
BASIC AMENITIES   The three
housing fixtures thought
necessary to make houses
reasonable to live in - an inside
lavatory, bathroom and hot-
water system.
BEHAVIOUR   Actions.
BIAS   One-sided or exaggerated
interpretation of information.
CENSUS   An official count of the
population of Britain which
takes place every ten years.
CLAIMANTS' UNION   A union
organized to protect the interests
of people who claim and have to
rely on Welfare State benefits.
COMMUNE   A group of adults and
children living closely together
like a family but who are not
necessarily related to each other.
COMMUNITY   A group of people
who live in the same neighbourhood and who share a similar way
of life.
CONSUMER   A user of goods and
products.
CROSS SECTION   A group of
people, varied in age, sex and
background.
DIRECT ACTION   A form of
protest which is usually illegal
and carried out to demonstrate
disagreement with an official
policy or decision. Direct action
can be peaceful or violent.
DISCRIMINATION   The practice
of treating people differently
and unfairly - usually to the
advantage of some and
disadvantage of others.

ENVIRONMENT Everything that surrounds us and influences the way we live.

EUTHANASIA Helping someone who is in great pain or suffering to a gentle and easy death by an overdose or underdose of drugs.

EXTENDED FAMILY Two or three generations of relatives living under the same roof or closely together and dependent on each other for help, contact and support.

FACT A thing that is known to be true.

GANG A group of people who have a lot in common and go around together. Often used as a term of abuse by adult and 'respectable' society because it's associated with delinquent behaviour.

GROUP A number of people who have certain characteristics in common.

INTERVIEW To question someone to find out about their ideas.

INVESTIGATION A study or inquiry into some aspect of human behaviour.

KIBBUTZ A community of people (not necessarily related) living and working closely together - found in Israel.

MORTGAGE A loan of money from a building society to buy a house.

NATIONAL INSURANCE CONTRIBUTIONS A sum of money taken off a person's wages by the state while he/she is working to provide money to live on when he/she is not working e.g. unemployed, sick, having a baby or retired.

OPINION A belief that is not necessarily based on fact, evidence or proof.

POLLUTION Waste, noise or smell which has unpleasant or destructive effects on the environment.

PREJUDICE One-sided and often rather narrow-minded opinion about someone or something. Usually firmly believed but without much thought or evidence.

PUBLIC OPINION The generally agreed views of the majority of ordinary people - very likely to be influenced by the mass media.

QUESTIONNAIRE A series of questions carefully worked out and usually written down to study the opinions or behaviour of a group of people.

RACE A group of people who share the same inherited physical characteristics affecting skin colour, physical appearance and stature.

ROLE The part we play in each of the various social groups we belong to.

ROLE CONFLICT Because we play a variety of different roles in different groups there can be times when an individual finds two or more of his/her roles at odds with each other. This is called role conflict.

SERVICE INDUSTRY An organization employing people to provide services for people (e.g. meals, beauty care, medical facilities) as distinct from employing people to make things.

SEX A biological term to mean being male or female.

SEX ROLES The characteristic behaviour expected of males and females in society. Largely learned behaviour which varies between different societies and at different periods of history.

SOCIAL CLASS The distinction made between larger groups of people in our society based on how much wealth and power they have, and what kinds of jobs they do.

SOCIETY The collective name given to all the people who live together in the same country or nation.

SOCIOLOGY The study of human behaviour.

SOCIOLOGISTS Someone who studies human behaviour.

STATISTICS A series of figures which record specific information.

STATUS A person's standing or rank in society. How he/she is rated in relation to other people.

STEREOTYPE A fixed and exaggerated idea about someone or something. Arrived at by applying the (usually) bad characteristics of one or two individuals to all members of the same group.

SUPPLEMENTARY BENEFITS Money you can claim from the state if you haven't enough to live on.

TRADE UNIONS Organizations to protect the interests and rights of workers and to try to improve their pay and working conditions.

WELFARE STATE The system of social and financial benefits provided by the state and paid for by contributions made by working people.

YOUTH MOVEMENT A group of young people who for a period of time share common interests, clothes, attitudes and behaviour, so much so that they can be identified as members of the same group.

USEFUL ADDRESSES

Advisory Centre for Education, 32 Trumpington Street, Cambridge

Age Concern, Bernard Sunley House, 60 Pitcairn Road, Mitcham, Surrey.

Anti-Apartheid Movement, 9 Charlotte Street, London W1

BBC, Broadcasting House, Portland Place, London W1

Census Division, Customer Services Section, Titchfield, Hants

Central Statistical Office, Great George Street, London SW1P 3AQ

Child Poverty Action Group, 1 Macklin Street, Drury Lane, London WC2

Children's Rights Workshop, 73 Balfour Street, London

Chinese Chargé d'Affaires, Cultural Section, 31 Portland Place, London W1

Christian Aid, 2 Sloane Gardens, London SW1

Citizens' Advice Bureau, 1 Macklin Street, Drury Lane, London WC2

Claimants' Union, Dame Collet House, Ben Jonson Road, London E1

Commonwealth Institute, Kensington High Street, London W8

Community Relations Commission, 15/16 Bedford Street, London WC2E 9HY

Community Service Volunteers, 237 Pentonville Road, London N1

Conservative Party, 32 Smith Square, London SW1

Consumers' Association, 14 Buckingham Street, London WC2

Department of Education and Science, Elizabeth House, 39 York Road, London SE1 7PLX

Department of Employment, Orphanage Road, Watford, Herts WD1 1PJ

Department of the Environment, St Christopher House, Southwark Street, London SE1 0TE

Department of Health and Social Security, 14 Russell Square, London WC1B 5EP

Equal Opportunities Commission, Overseas House, Quay Street, Manchester

Family Planning Association, 27-35 Mortimer Street, London W1

Gypsy Council, 343 Garrat Lane, London SW18

Help the Aged, Denham Street, London W1

HMSO, Atlantic House, Holborn Viaduct, London EC1

HMSO Bookshop, 45 High Holborn, London WC1

Home Office, Whitehall, London SW1

Joint Council for the Welfare of Immigrants, Toynbee Hall, Commercial Street, London E1

Independent Broadcasting Authority, 70 Brompton Road, London SW3

Israel Government Tourist Office, 59 St James's Street, London SW1

Labour Party, Transport House, Smith Square, London SW1

Liberal Party, National Liberal Club, 1 Whitehall Place, London SW1

National Abortion Campaign, 30 Camden Road, London

National Children's Bureau, 8 Wakley Street, London EC1

National Council for Civil Liberties, 186 Kings Cross Road, London WC1

National Marriage Guidance Council, Herbert Gray College, Little Church Street, Rugby

National Society for the Prevention of Cruelty to Children, 1 Ridinghouse Street, London W1

National Union of Railwaymen, Unity House, Euston Road, London NW1

National Union of School Students, 3 Endsleigh Street, London WC1

National Union of Teachers, Hamilton House, Mabledon Place, London WC1

Office of Population Censuses and Surveys, St Katherine's House, Kingsway, London WC2

Oxfam, 274 Banbury Road, Oxford

Race Relations Board, 5 Lower Belgrave Street, London SW1

Romany Guild, c/o Tom Lee, Caravan Site, Folly Lane, Walthamstow, London E17

Scottish National Party, 14A Manor Place, Edinburgh

Shelter, 86 The Strand, London WC2R 0EQ

Society for Anglo-Chinese Understanding, 152 Camden High Street, London NW7

South African Embassy, South Africa House, Trafalgar Square, London WC2

Trades Union Congress, Great Russell Street, London WC1

Transport and General Workers' Union, Woodbury, 218 Green Lane, Finsbury Park, London N4

United Kingdom Immigrants' Advisory Service, St George's Churchyard, Bloomsbury Way, London WC1

United Nations Information Service, 14/15 Stratford Place, London W1

Welsh National Party, 8 Heoly Frenhines, Cardiff

Women's Liberation Workshop, 38 Earlham Street, London WC2

Women's Research and Resources Centre, 158 North Gower Street, London NW1

Working Women's Charter Group, 16 Crookham Road, London SW16